The Church

An Organic Picture of Its Life and Mission

The Church

An Organic Picture of Its Life and Mission

By

ROBERT BROW

WILLIAM B. EERDMANS PUBLISHING COMPANY
GRAND RAPIDS, MICHIGAN

Acknowledgments

Paul, apostle, first practiced what I have written

Roland Allen, priest, missionary, reminded us what Paul did

Watchman Nee, prisoner for Christ, taught much about apostles, elders, and the Christian life

C. S. Lewis, English professor, set an example of readable Christian writing

Peggy Tracy, journalist, neighbor, corrected many obscurities

Ann Benoit, secretary, housewife, typed the manuscript and gave much encouragement

Mollie, partner, mother of my children, made this book possible

Contents

One

Sixties and Seventies

The most visible part of the church in the 1960s is self-criticism. No longer do Christians sit in judgment on others, or rebuke the ways of the wicked world. "Woe is me! I am undone. I am a man of unclean lips" is what Isaiah felt when he had seen a vision of God. Today the church seems to be saying "Woe to us as a church. We are outdated. Our message is irrelevant in a world that has left us behind."

Nineteen sixty-three was the year of *Honest to God,* Bishop J. A. T. Robinson's self-criticism of the message of his church.[1] The same year Pierre Berton's *The Comfortable Pew* provided the first case of an avowed agnostic's being hired by a Christian church to castigate its doctrine and practices. Its success was tremendous, at least among the faithful, and cries of outrage helped to fan the flames. One minister called it "an ecclesiastical *Fanny Hill*"; another invited Berton to preach in his Anglican (Episcopal) church.[2]

The United Church of Canada immediately followed suit with a more modest invitation to half a dozen writers "not noted for their pious forbearance" to throw their rocks at the church. One of these was duly impressed by the fact that "only the strong

---

[1] Robinson, *Honest to God* (Philadelphia: Westminster, 1963).

[2] See also William Kilbourn (ed.), *The Restless Church: A Response to The Comfortable Pew,* introduction.

offer themselves for martyrdom," which was perhaps what the invitation was meant to prove.[3]

The mood of self-flagellation has taken strongest root in the Roman Catholic Church, especially since Pope John XXIII and the Second Vatican Council. Instead of building prickly defenses, its theologians, orders, and laymen have begun a remorseless program of questioning even the most sacred institutions. By 1967 the mood had become a flood, and for the first time an international gathering of Roman Catholic laymen dared to criticize openly the decisions of the Pope himself.[4]

Seven main directions of self-criticism are evident. First, in the tradition of *Honest to God,* is the suggestion that the message of the Christian gospel is dated, unintelligible to modern man, and in need of reformulation in space-age terms. Bishop Robinson was quickly followed by those who thought that it was quite inadequate merely to tinker with the creeds. What was needed was an acceptance of the fact that God himself is dead, and Christians are really better off without him.

Second, and much older, is the problem of church unity. "The sin of our divisions" is the main concern of the World Council of Churches, and a large part of assembly and committee time in the Protestant churches is devoted to the practical problems of administrative unification. Previous church union schemes such as those in southern India and Canada were more like trial balloons, launched in countries where Protestant church history was hardly a century old. In the sixties large, prosperous churches began to struggle seriously to unite across major historical cleavages; and at the same time the possibility of eventual union with the Roman Catholic Church came into clear focus.

The third area, the need for social involvement, had been championed in Britain since F. D. Maurice and the Christian Socialist Movement. The political implications of the kingdom of God on earth was a favorite theme of the American Unitar-

---

[3] *Why the Sea is Boiling Hot: A Symposium on the Church and the World.*

[4] October 1967 Third World Congress for the Lay Apostolate. In the same Canadian tradition of *The Comfortable Pew* is Paul T. Harris (ed.), *Brief to the Bishops: Canadian Catholic Laymen Speak Their Minds.*

ians and Modernists. Now in the sixties the church's self-criticism on social matters has become strident with the explosive issues of civil rights and war in Vietnam. It is one thing to feel that the church should be doing more for bringing about the day of peace and brotherhood on earth; it is quite another to have millions of ordinary Christians involved directly in racial hatred and a war that very few either understand or even want.

A fourth, more sophisticated self-criticism has come to the fore in Harvey Cox's *The Secular City*. Cox's problem is not how the church is going to speak and act in relation to social problems caused by political forces. He suggests that the very concept of the church as a religious institution is wrong. Christians in the urbanized technopolis of the 1970s must be ready to be utterly secular. They should be thoroughly *of* the world as well as *in* the world. Instead of preaching from outside, they must live and exert an influence from the inside. Rather than repent, they must be responsible and mature, which does not mean traditional Victorian morality.

Fifth, laymen are disillusioned, dissatisfied, disoriented because they cannot see where they fit in the life of their plush new suburban churches. They no longer accept the minister as one of the three sources of all wisdom together with the village teacher and doctor. A hundred years ago the minister was usually the most educated man in the community; now he is surrounded by scientific, technological, sociological, and commercial experts in their own right. The laymen of the sixties know that they know something, whereas the minister's theological science has become so uncertain that he hardly has a right to speak. In the past he could at least be expected to be a competent administrator, and the flock could agree to follow. Now there are laymen by the hundreds who belong to the new breed of executives. These men are paid according to their ability to get things done efficiently. In the church they are expected to give their money for inefficient projects and to waste their time in committee activities and trivialities, things that would never be tolerated in a business corporation.

The 1960s have seen the growth of a powerful charismatic movement parallel to and sometimes overlapping the administrative dissatisfaction. Although some ministers have been

11

prominent in this, it is largely an expression of spiritual hunger on the part of Christians hoping to recover the spiritual emphasis of the New Testament. Bored with strawberry festivals, interminable committees, and superficial togetherness, men and women are willing to spend whole evenings in prayer, Bible study, and fellowship at a very deep level. The attention given to this movement has usually been focused on speaking in tongues and on its notable failures, but to emphasize only this is as shallow as to ignore the life of the New Testament churches because they spoke in tongues and had the admitted Judases — Ananias and Sapphira, Demas, and the rest. The point is that this is a genuine movement of self-criticism that is dissatisfied with substandard Christian living and believes that somehow the Holy Spirit is still relevant to the twentieth century.

The seventh movement of self-criticism is found among the ordained ministers of all the major denominations, as well as the priests of the Roman Catholic Church. Such self-criticism is inevitable in view of the other six: theological confusion, interchurch dialogue, strong feelings of concern on social issues, the secularization of everything except the church, laymen who make no bones about their disrespect, and a charismatic movement that is divisive, confusing, and at the same time a reminder of what happened in the New Testament. All these things have produced deep self-searching among thousands of men, who at one time thought they had been genuinely called by God to serve in the ministry. Their self-criticism has been silent. They have seen some writing on the wall, but it is not to be shared with their church members, or even with their fellow ministers. Their very life is involved. Countries complain of a "brain drain," but the flight from the ministry is of staggering proportions. If we took the last twenty graduating classes of any well-known Protestant seminary, and checked how many are actually in regular parish ministry, the dropout rate would be astonishing. Disquieting surveys have indicated that few ministers would recommend the ministry to their sons, and that many would in fact make a change to another profession if they had half a chance.

What then of the seventies? Surely we cannot continue our exhaustive self-criticism for another harrowing ten years. Christians are duly convinced that the church is in a mess; their leaders are more dubious about its present state than they are. Admittedly we live in an age of revolution and the church is left on the shelf; we face a life and death crisis, etc., *ad nauseam*. But where do we go from here and how do we get there? That is the question that lies behind our self-criticism, and this book is a small contribution towards an answer.

I have no intention of adding to the works of flagellation. My aim is to suggest that the organic life of the first century of the church is equally suited to the twentieth century. In the words of Marshall McLuhan "the medium is the message," and in a very real sense the church of Jesus Christ is the message of Jesus Christ. If the church could be freed to live as it lived in the first two or three centuries, many of the problems that we have noted would be solved in a genuinely radical fashion, *from the root*.

Our method, then, is to look again at the original and perennial forms of the church as a living organism — a body, in the sense of that term in Paul's epistles. In the case of each form or activity, we shall first try to recapture the atmosphere of the New Testament, and then see how this developed in helpful or unhelpful ways in church history and in various denominations. In some cases this should result in practical suggestions for the 1970s. Having seen the church from the inside in several countries and three or four different denominational traditions, I have no doubt that what is alive is worth conserving. I would like to convince the doubters and the self-critical that Jesus Christ intends to keep building his church, and that the gates of hell are even less likely to prevail than in the past. Where criticism is necessary, this is not directed at any particular denomination, since I delight in the one church of Jesus Christ, and the reader will discern that I long to see every part enjoying the richness of the whole.

Two

Synagogues and Churches

We shall begin with local churches. These are the basic units of organic church life, the irreducible minimum necessary in order for Christianity to exist. We are not speaking of buildings, since Christians have often done without them. Nor do we mean elaborate organizations with hundreds of members. Where two or three are gathered together in the name of Jesus Christ, there he is. Christians might meet in a concentration camp; and they could lack hymnbooks and account books, even Bibles, sacraments, and any formal connection with other churches, but they would be recognized by Jesus Christ as a local church meeting in his name.

The root origin of these local churches is best seen in the transition from Jewish synagogues to Christian congregations. At first all Christians were Jews, and they belonged to synagogues. Within these synagogue congregations, the Christians began to declare that Jesus was the Christ. Inevitably there were soon synagogues that recognized Jesus as the Christ, organized alongside those where the question was still open. Gradually it dawned on these Jewish Christians that their Lord was the one who had been promised as the light to the Gentiles, and so they found themselves taking non-Jews into their membership. The book of Acts and the epistles of Paul illustrate the tremendous struggles that took place as Christian and non-Christian Jews discussed this matter.

Forty years later the break was complete, and men had to choose between being Christian or Jewish, since they could no longer be both. Today the wheel has come a full circle. Churches can easily cease to be Christian, while some synagogues come remarkably close to being churches.

Synagogues were ideally suited for the momentous New Testament decisions concerning the Messiah. Dating back to the exile five hundred years earlier, they are the first example of the modern concept of the freedom of religion. Every Jew was free to belong or not to belong to a synagogue. In any large city he would have a choice of several organizations with a rich variety of Pharisee, Sadducee, Zealot, and Essene emphases. Synagogue government was by elected elders, and there was no need of priests or even of a theologically trained rabbi. If no existing synagogue suited him, a Jew had only to find nine other men over thirteen years of age who would join with him to organize a new one.

We know that Jesus attended synagogues regularly. Although he was not a qualified rabbi, he was often given the freedom to preach (Luke 4:15f., 31, 33, 44; John 18:20). On his missionary journeys Paul always attended one of the local synagogues on the Sabbath day, and he too was usually asked if he had a word of exhortation to present (cf. Acts 9:20; 13:5, 14, 43; 14:1; 17:1, 2, 10, 17; 18:4). There were thus ready-made preaching centers in all the major cities to give a first hearing to the preaching of Jesus. Since these were free democratic institutions, there could of course be opposition to the message; and freedom to preach could be terminated, as was often the case with Paul. The point was that each synagogue and every individual in it had an opportunity to make an informed decision concerning the Messiah.

In the case of the Bereans of Macedonia (Acts 17:10-12) we find a whole synagogue convinced by Paul's preaching and by their own careful study of the Scriptures. This may have been the first case of an entire synagogue that moved over to a Christ-believing theology. In most places, however, the time soon came when a separate Christian synagogue had to be formed. This happened in Corinth, where the new church began meeting right next to the synagogue, and one of the first converts was Crispus, who had been its leader (Acts 18:1-18). In Ephesus Aquila and Priscilla had attended the synagogue as a kind of Christian advance party. When Paul returned, the new Christ-believing synagogue was organized within three months in a rented hall (Acts 18:19f.; 19:1-9).

There are only a few examples in the book of Acts, but obviously this movement of Christian synagogues forming in each city went on in waves across the Roman world and far to the east along the trade routes to India and China. The fact that only ten male adult members were needed meant that churches could mushroom as new believers were added. As Roland Allen pointed out in his writings, elders could begin functioning immediately, no foreign priests or organizers had to be imported to stifle their growth, and there was no need to send off promising young men for college and seminary training before a native ministry could be ordained.

The first Christian synagogues were naturally organized in the same way as those that preceded them. In Jerusalem the apostles did not wish to be involved in the responsibilities of local eldership, so they asked the Church to elect elders to deal with their own administrative problems. It is usually assumed that Stephen and the others appointed for this were "deacons," but Luke does not say this, and the functions performed by these men are typical of synagogue elders. In any case by the time of the Council of Jerusalem reported in Acts 15, the Jerusalem Church was governed by elders in the usual way. As Paul and Barnabas founded new churches in Galatia, they immediately organized them as self-governing synagogues under the leadership of their own elders (Acts 14:23). This method of government was so natural that Luke does not even mention the appointment of elders in Ephesus, although they were obviously functioning a few months later when Paul called them to Miletus for a final briefing (Acts 20:17). After a major evangelistic campaign in Crete, Titus was left behind to make certain that every town had a properly functioning church with suitable elders (Titus 1:5).

In addition to elders for its government, a synagogue might

have one or more paid or unpaid servants (Greek, *diakonos*) to help with maintenance and other duties. As churches grew in size they had deacons for the same purposes. As we shall see later, the distinction between elders and deacons is that the former constitute the governing board, while the latter execute the secretarial and domestic duties of the society.

In Jewish synagogues one of the elders often became the leader or president of the board of elders. He provided a center of administration, a postal address for communications, and the leadership continuity that a committee cannot give. Luke mentions Jairus (Luke 8:49), Crispus (Acts 18:8), and Sosthenes (Acts 18:17), as men who had this function.[1] Similarly in Christian synagogues there was a natural development of the Bishop from among the elder bishops. Particularly when persecution devastated the churches, it was essential to have one man with executive responsibility. At first he was only one of the elders, who was asked to act by the others when they could not meet as a committee. As we shall see in the next chapter, his power increased; and the leader of a city church eventually became bishop for a whole group of churches in the surrounding district.

The greatest difference from Jewish synagogues was the admission of women to Christian synagogue membership. Whereas first-century Jewish synagogues had no place for women — even as members — Christian women were from the first accepted into full membership. Some of them became deaconesses, like Phoebe of Cenchrea (Rom. 16:1). Paul gives Timothy the qualifications of women to serve the churches right after describing the kind of men who should be appointed (I Tim. 3:11).

There were also prophetesses like Philip's four unmarried daughters (Acts 21:9), though it appears that Paul did not consider that a woman should continue to prophesy or teach or lead in public prayer after marriage (I Cor. 14:33-36; 1 Tim. 2:11-15). This may explain why women were not elected to

---

[1] The original identity of elders and bishops was demonstrated by Bishop J. B. Lightfoot in the appendix on "The Christian Ministry," *Saint Paul's Epistle to the Philippians*, pp. 181-269.

eldership. Elders were, as their name indicates, older, experienced, respected men in the community; and since most women
were married at an early age, few could qualify. The church
is still discussing how the new place of women in twentieth-
century society relates to the question of ordination in the
church. We can note in passing that ordination as we discuss it
today was not the question. Laying on of hands was then used
for a wide variety of appointments, whereas we limit it today
to a particular kind of minister. It is function, not ordination,
that is the real question, but a discussion of this is better post-
poned until after a detailed study of functions in the church
(see Ch. XV).

We conclude this brief look at the synagogue organization of
local churches by seeing how it relates to the growth of our
denominations. A rudimentary Jewish synagogue could be an
informal weekly meeting of ten men to read the Law and the
Prophets, to sing or say the Psalms, and to pray. A fully
developed synagogue would have a board of elders with the
equivalent of a managing director, paid servants, a properly
qualified teaching rabbi, a large community day school, and the
elaborate buildings that were required.[2] In time synagogues
naturally grouped themselves with like-minded meetings in
other cities. The grouping might be a loose fellowship or a
rigidly organized international body. Some of these groupings
are mentioned by Luke: "Then some of those who belonged to
the synagogue of the Freedmen (as it was called), and of the
Cyrenians, and of the Alexandrians, and of those from Cilicia
and Asia, arose and disputed with Stephen" (Acts 6:9).
Similarly Christian churches were bound to associate together
in various national, sociological, or ecclesiastical patterns.

Once churches begin to organize groups and conferences,
strong differences of opinion arise. A grouping may become so
large that it genuinely feels that it must be the original deposi-
tory of the truth. Its rules of operation, its hierarchical structure,
and its stability tend to make other newer groupings look
spurious. This happened in the congregations connected with the
empire's capital church in Rome. In terms of numbers there

---

2 See Isaac Levy, *The Synagogue: Its History and Function.*

were equally impressive groupings around the ecumenical patriarch of Constantinople and the Nestorian and Jacobite patriarchs of the Syriac-speaking churches of the east.

Other Christians are temperamentally suspicious of such vast power structures, or they may need to form new organizations to stress what God has taught them. There will always be Montanists, Waldensians, Lollards, Hussites, Friends, Brethren, and their successors to rebuke and teach the institutional church.[3] Other groupings will associate for geographical and social reasons. As the uprooted immigrants from Europe arrived in the United States and Canada they integrated best where the first generation could worship in their own ethnic churches. Their grandchildren were sufficiently acclimated to branch out and choose a congregation for other reasons.

It is time that Christians learned that their brethren in a feudal state or a tribal culture or in Communist countries are unlikely to organize themselves in the same way as in a fast-moving *laissez-faire* republic. Even within one country it seems unreasonable to enforce musical conformity, for example. Let every Christian feel at home whether he prefers the organ or the saxophone, whether he wants to clap his hands or beat his drum or sit stiffly in bourgeois decorum.[4] Obviously there has to be a wide range of church forms to provide for the variety of human preferences. Ideally one might like to see one single united church, but it would have to be big enough to allow every type of Christian the full freedom to express his faith in whatever way best suited him. This quality of bigness is unlikely to be found this side of the City of God. Meanwhile Christian maturity must be evidenced by a recognition of variety, a genuine respect for differences, and the deliberate avoidance of pressure to make others conform to one's own denominational pattern. Conformity to Christ by all means, but this has nothing whatever to do with one's own particular tradition.

If we believe in truth and in the freedom to decide, we must

---

[3] *The Oxford Dictionary of the Christian Church* gives basic information and bibliography for each of these.

[4] For evidence that theological reasons are a minor explanation of our denominations, see H. Richard Niebuhr, *The Social Sources of Denominationalism.*

also allow the freedom so evident in the first-century Jewish synagogues: freedom for an unlettered man to be heard, freedom to reject a teacher who does not conform to God's Word, freedom to form a new synagogue if necessary, freedom to associate or not to associate with other groupings, freedom for men to be different and to be themselves, freedom to argue and to disagree.

Three

Bishops and Popes

Protestants of the non-Episcopal sort have usually assumed that bishops and popes are the wicked fruits of medievalism or priestly pretensions. That the ordered hierarchy of priests and bishops under one pope was part and parcel of European feudalism is a fact. That the Protestant Reformation abandoned the hierarchical idea is by no means proved. That many Protestant clergy long for its restoration is evident in the ecumenical movement.

We have seen the transition from Jewish synagogues governed by lay elders to Christian churches grouped under city church bishops. When bishops meet together in council, one of them becomes first among equals, and if he is elected for life he naturally attains a higher status. At its worst the complete system can be caricatured as: Christ established Peter, who was succeeded by the popes, who chose bishops, who made some men priests. The priests then make certain people Christians by baptizing them and feeding them with the sacraments.

When the Lutheran Reformation and the English Methodists substituted superintendents for bishops there was no change in the hierarchical principle. Actually there was not even much of a verbal change since the Greek word *episkopos* literally means superintendent. Anglicans retained the previous system intact, but instead of one pope, appointed two archbishops. This helped to clarify the point that there was no need to have one figurehead for the whole of Europe or even for one country and also made the old English game of balance of power easier to play.

Presbyterians reverted to government by elders, but with the stress on a highly educated ministry, elders were no match for the minister, who soon received more deference and authority than the old priests. With the best will in the world it was still impossible to prevent the hierarchical principle from re-establishing itself. "Moderator" sounded less impressive than a "Pope" or "Archbishop," and by changing frequently he could be prevented from learning the ways of power; but then the office of stated clerk provided hierarchical continuity. A similar situation had occurred in the Middle Ages when the head deacon, who was basically an administrative assistant, gradually became so powerful under changing bishops that the position of archdeacon was filled by a priest often next in line for the bishopric.

The Episcopal system can operate with a considerable degree of democracy, so that in some countries the Anglican bishop really has very little power to act apart from his diocesan council. In practice there is often very little difference between the Episcopal and Presbyterian types of organization, especially in the younger churches. This explains the ease with which church union schemes can unite Episcopal and non-Episcopal churches, once the thorny problem of the meaning of the act of unification is clarified.[1] Organizationally there is evidently no insuperable problem in further acts of unification with Roman Catholic hierarchies. It is interesting that in the United States and some parts of Europe and Asia there are Roman Catholic bishops with over-lapping dioceses.[2] In Britain, for example,

---

[1] Basically the question is whether the act is a reordination, or a full mutual acceptance, or as in South India a provisional acceptance on the understanding that all future ordinations will be by bishops in the apostolic succession.

[2] Uniat churches such as the Maronites, Antiochene Syrians, Alexandrine Copts, and various Byzantine groups retain their language, rites, and canon law under their own bishops in full communion with the Church of Rome. (See *Oxford Dictionary of the Christian Church* under "Uniat.")

there seems to be no great problem on the part of the Roman Catholics in accepting the Anglican bishops with their Prayer Book, married clergy, and canon law, functioning in overlapping dioceses together with the existing Roman Catholic bishops. The point is that the problems of church union are basically theological, economic, and emotional, not organizational.

The greatest divergence from the hierarchical system was among the Baptists, Mennonites, and Congregational groups, who insisted on the complete independence of each local congregation. A large addition to the Congregational system of government in the twentieth century has been the phenomenal growth of the independent Pentecostal churches.[3] The stronghold of true Congregationalism is the possession of the title deeds of the church building and the right of the congregation to call and dismiss a pastor without pressure from any other authority. This means that conferences of such churches must be for consultation and fellowship only. If functions like the training and ordination of ministers are centralized, the essential Congregational principle is lost. Inevitably there is constant pressure from the executives of the church hierarchy to surrender local autonomy in order to give greater strength together. When churches are no longer free to dispose of their property or change their affiliation to another conference or call the minister of their choice, then they are basically more Presbyterian than Congregational. When in a Presbyterian system executive power continues for any length of time in one man by virtue of his office, whether at the presbytery or the general assembly level, then for all practical purposes there is a transition to an Episcopal system.

The gradations of hierarchical organization may be set out as follows, depending on the exact point where ultimate authority resides:

CONGREGATION　　All full members have equal unrestricted authority at the congregational level.

---

[3] In South America the Pentecostalists have already outstripped the other Protestant groups, and in some areas they challenge the Roman churches in effective membership.

ELDERS	Once appointed, the local church elders govern the church without a veto from the congregation or superior authority.
SYNOD	Authority resides in the duly constituted representatives of a group of churches. Usually the local congregation is restricted in its disposal of property and the calling of ministers.
BISHOP	As head of a group of churches, an individual, whether he is called bishop, superintendent, or any other name, exercises authority over them without restriction from above.
NATIONAL BODY	The ultimate authority for all churches within one country resides in the duly constituted representatives of those churches. Representatives may be bishops, ministers, laymen, or any combination of these.
POPE	Ultimate authority to appoint bishops across national boundaries resides in one man by virtue of his office.

In the modern church situation the exact point of ultimate authority is usually obscured by a large number of checks and counterchecks. At the time of the Reformation the Anglican Church changed its ultimate authority from papal to national. On the theory that all Englishmen were Anglicans and all were represented in Parliament, the Church of England found, and still finds, itself subject to Parliament. Its bishops are appointed by the Prime Minister, who might be an atheist. In the United States both Anglican and Methodist Episcopalians use democratic methods to elect their bishops, and give them strong executive powers similar to a United States president. Congregational churches have tended towards synodical government, and have easily joined Presbyterian-type groups in church union schemes. Many non-Episcopal churches have very authoritarian bishops among them. Even anticlerical groups like the Brethren assemblies can be invisibly dominated by a powerful personality.

Since Pope John XXIII the Roman Catholic Church has been engaged in a tremendous struggle to rearrange its centers of authority. The supranational power of the pope and curia is being challenged by the bishops. In the parishes laymen are beginning to erode the absolute authority of the parish priests. Among Protestants there are slightly less obvious battles in every major denomination. As effective authority moves from the session to presbytery, from parish council to diocesan council, from a bishop or superintendent to an elected body, or from a hierarchy back to local churches, the whole countenance of a denomination may change. Like the tides there is always a movement of ebb and flow; and as long as God is God, man's worst may often turn out for good. Since the days of Wycliffe many laymen and some of the more evangelical ministers have bewailed the fact that the hierarchy and its "organization men" dominate the scene and force the Holy Spirit to find a home among the newer sects. It is possible that the tide may have already turned, and the day of true local church Congregationalism may appear as unexpectedly as it did in the early apostolic churches.

Apart from that hope, what can we conclude from this dismal survey? Primarily that denominational names are deceptive. They do not indicate the true structure of the church, which is organic. Ultimate power may reside in the least likely hands. Second, it should be recognized that a degree of hierarchical development is almost inevitable, however much one may long for the simplicity of the early churches. Unrestricted government by all members at the local level has rarely proved effective. Within the organic church — the true body of Christ — and around it as it exists on earth, denominations are inevitable. Third, I suggest that at the local level elders have functioned acceptably, whether they are called the session, the parish council, the deacons, or the church board. In God's economy it seems that local churches with elders are the essence of the visible church.

Beyond these generalities we may find that the structures and levels of authority that seem so basic to our denominations are in fact matters of temperament rather than theology; and the surprising thing is that God blesses even in the systems which we find most distasteful.

Four

Groups and Tribes

Bishops and popes, hierarchies and conferences, denominational structures, mergers, and splits — these are what men see
of the church; these are what is reported in *Time* and *The
Times*. From God's point of view they are uninteresting. There
is joy in heaven only when the prodigal comes home, the sinner
becomes a saint, superstitious terror turns to joy unspeakable.
This is church growth. It influences nations and creates civilization on a vast scale, but at its growing edges it has no news
value. And yet no man can say anything relevant about the
church unless he has seen as God sees. Faith is intensely
personal. Its origin is as invisible as the falling of a speck of
dandelion seed. In time the leaves will appear and yellow flowers
will cover the lawn, but the actual moment of conception is
unpredictable. Church growth can only be observed well after
God's work has been done.

It is a commonplace that the foundations of western European
civilization are Christian. They go back to the conversion of
savage tribes that had pillaged across the forests of Europe and
Britain. These numbered a few hundred thousand; we now count
millions of equally savage tribesmen who have become Christians in the past hundred years. In South America, across Central Africa, in the hills of India, Burma, and China, in the
islands of Southeast Asia there has been astonishing church

growth. Whereas the Moslems and Hindus and the educated Confucianists and Buddhists have been virtually untouched, primitive animistic tribes have responded in vast numbers. We must beware of despising what God has not despised, and, after all, such were the roots from which we have come. Political signs of new life have appeared in the independence movements that have added dozens of countries to the United Nations. All these are only the beginning of long-term developments that will be no less significant than the conversion of the pagan tribes of Europe.

As soon as politics and the conversion of tribes and large numbers added to the churches are mentioned, we need to face some important objections. Is not faith an individual matter? Are not many of these baptisms for economic advantages or other wrong motives? How many of these so-called Christians are true believers? What evidences of Christian character indicate that this is really a work of God? What about all the tares among the wheat? Less worthy of consideration is the stupidity that asks: "But have these people read our books, understood our philosophy, and thought out their problems as we have?"

At this point we need to make a clear distinction between two things that are inseparable. On the one hand there is a visible community, the people of God, and on the other there is an inner core, known only to God, of those who are truly his. The Old Testament prophets knew that there were the ungodly, the sons of Belial, the wicked, the uncircumcised in heart among God's people. Paul explains that "he is not a real Jew who is one outwardly, nor is the true circumcision something external and physical. He is a Jew who is one inwardly, and real circumcision is a matter of the heart, spiritual and not literal" (Rom. 2:28f.). Jesus indicated that many would be deceived about their own state before God: "Not everyone who says to me, 'Lord, Lord,' shall enter the kingdom of heaven, but he who does the will of my Father who is in heaven. In that day many will say to me, 'Lord, Lord, did we not prophesy in your name, and cast out demons in your name, and do many mighty works in your name?' And then will I declare to them, 'I never knew you; depart from me, you evildoers.'"

As we shall see in the next chapter, denominations vary as

to the conditions they impose for baptism and membership. Some missionaries make stringent rules, extending the time of preparation and observation for years, to try to prevent any unconverted from entering the church. Others are happy to sprinkle water on untaught multitudes to take in as many as possible. With the best efforts the most carefully schooled convert can turn out to be a Judas, and on the other hand true faith may suddenly blossom among those who came in untaught and with the worst of motives.

Let us imagine a typical tribal situation and see how the decisions are made that result in church growth. The tribe is a social unit with its own unwritten dialect. They have some contact with the neighboring civilization in the market town, and some of the men know the trade language. The only schooling is the tribal lore, and the tribal elders are men of deep wisdom. Their decisions become law, and offenders are severely punished.

Now a missionary arrives, learns the language, and gains the confidence of the people. The first converts who burn their fetishes and reject the spiritual control of the witch doctor face bitter persecution. Gradually the elders find themselves discussing the questions. Shall we or shall we not become Christians? What will be the effect on our crops and our hunting? If evil spirits cause sickness, how shall we manage without the witch doctor? If we become Christians, education will come to our tribe, but what about our tribal wars, and our drinking feasts?

One day, unknown to the missionary, the elders decide to become Christians, that it will be good for their tribe to change. Now growing numbers start asking to be prepared for baptism. Whatever conditions are required the candidates will sincerely try to meet them. The older men may decide to delay because they cannot quit drinking or abandon their several wives, but they will encourage the younger men to take the step.

At this point much depends on the work of the missionaries and the church workers whom they have trained. If they are wise they will first teach the elders to read and write and to maintain their tribal authority, even though this may take longer than turning the young men into upstart know-it-alls. If they have learned from Roland Allen, they will appoint local leaders immediately so that the churches can be self-governing from the beginning.[1] If they have learned from Donald Mc-Gavran, they will encourage the movement to go on, without requiring long periods of preparation for baptism — the baptisms in the New Testament were all immediate, without any time to test the quality of the lives of the converts.[2] If the missionaries believe in the Bible as God's appointed Word for the church, they will press on with Bible translation, doing all they can to teach every Christian family at home and in short-term Bible schools. If there is an emphasis on prayer and spiritual life and true heart experience, then many of the converts will become men of God and the fruits in changed lives will be beautifully impressive.

If, however, the tribal structure is carelessly torn down and missionaries become colonial paternalists, if the Bible is not taught and spiritual life is negligible, then the tribe would have been better off without these misguided do-gooders. If the missionary insists on such high standards for baptism that only a very few are taken in and the remainder of the tribe is left untouched, perhaps less harm is done, but church growth remains negligible.

So far we have concentrated on church growth from tribal societies. This was the type of movement that produced European Christendom, and it is the most significant development in many parts of the world in the past century. A similar type of group decision occurred in India in the so-called mass movements. These might better be called group movements, since they are confined to particular caste groups, rather than to the masses as usually understood. Instead of being located in a compact territory like a tribe, caste groups are scattered in a large number of villages. Members of the shoemakers' caste, for example, might number from two to a dozen families per village, but they have a strong social unity. Marriages are confined to the caste, and caste elders exercise effective discipline. When the Christian gospel makes an impact on such groups,

---

[1] Roland Allen, *St. Paul's Missionary Methods, or Ours?* and *The Spontaneous Expansion of the Church.*

[2] Donald McGavran, *The Bridges of God; How Churches Grow;* and *Church Growth Bulletin.*

the process of decision and church membership is identical with what we have seen in a tribe. The difference is that the problems of organizing and shepherding churches are tremendous. With only a few families in each village, and these usually from a despised lower caste, effective self-governing churches have been rare.

In spite of the problems, some of these caste movements were impressive; and they produced probably 80 percent of the visible church in India. The economic changes that occurred and the rapid improvement in social status were first described by Bishop Pickett.[3] The long-term results still have to be seen. When we consider that the caste system had remained unchanged from father to son for twenty-five hundred years, the changes that have taken place in the hundred years since the group movements began are remarkable.

We must also consider the waves of growth and decline within a country or a group that has previously adopted the Christian faith as its predominant religion. The countries of southern Europe were Christianized in this sense about A.D. 500, Britain by A.D. 700, Russia three hundred years later. South America was subjugated with misguided zeal by 1600. These dates roughly mark the first wave of church growth across a continent, though within each country there were movements in individual tribes before that time.[4]

After this first wave there were tidal movements set up by the forces of degeneration and decline, which were followed again and again by revival and spiritual growth. In Britain, for example, one could list the advances with Anselm in the eleventh century, the Franciscans in the thirteenth, Wycliffe and the Lollards in the fourteenth, the reformers in the sixteenth, the Puritans in the seventeenth, Wesley in the eighteenth, and the evangelical and missionary movements in the nineteenth. It is unnecessary to chronicle the declines: that of our own day is still painfully with us. In the United States the ebb and flow of spiritual life is as well documented in the history of revivals and the figures of church membership as the stock

---

[3] J. W. Pickett, *Christian Mass Movements in India.*
[4] See Stephen Neill, *A History of Christian Missions.*

exchange is mirrored by the Dow-Jones index. Obviously with each advance there is much that is spurious. Hypocrites find it convenient to profess what others are experiencing, the blessing of the parents may have been eroded by the second or third generation, and of course the church will be invaded by business interests to make a profit from the newest religious fashion. In the declines the church is just as quickly abandoned even by her friends. Hypocrites, questioning children, business interests, even the sincere find it embarrassing to be associated with what is dying. The point is that there is a movement of ebb and flow within every so-called Christian country, and this movement is quite different in character from the first wave, when there was the turning from idols to the living God.

This ebb and flow means that the missions of the church must not only be interested in the first wave on the frontiers of Christendom, but also with revival and true religion where love has grown cold. If they fail at this point, the situation may deteriorate — as it did in Ephesus and Asia Minor and North Africa — to the point where no visible church remains. God longs to see revival and reformation, but he apparently prefers to have no church than one that carries the name of his Son but misrepresents his way, his truth, and his life. Wherever local churches begin to deviate and to die, they need mission. One of the tragedies of Protestantism has been the failure to have a theology of mission that includes the churches at home. It is not just the heathen overseas who need to be won. Pagans in the church may be nearer, but they are no easier to disciple. The Roman Catholic orders like the Jesuits, Dominicans, and Franciscans have been more realistic at this point. We will consider this further in Chapters XIII and XIV when we look at the relationship of the church to its missions.

Five

Baptism and Membership

Any club or society must have a membership criterion. Every group of members has a right to make conditions for the admission of other members. It also needs to decide under what conditions members should be expelled. In this sense any synagogue or local church, whether Anglican or Baptist, Roman Catholic or Pentecostal, Brethren or Friends, Salvation Army Citadel or Mormon Temple, must have a membership and it must have rules.

We are not discussing the question of belonging to the invisible church of God, since only Jesus Christ decides its membership and knows its extent. We are concentrating on the rules that are made to admit members to the privileges of local church membership.

In the first place, the less power an ordinary member has, the lower the standard of membership tends to be. When all authority is in the hands of a hierarchy of priests, membership can be given to any person who respects the organization and the priests who conduct its affairs. Membership need be suspended only if the authority of the priest is flouted. If, on the other hand, membership carries full voting rights, with authority over the church property and its ministers, as in many Baptist and Pentecostal churches, then the standards of membership are bound to be more selective. Only a man who believes aright and behaves, or better still is obviously indwelt by the Holy Spirit, has the right to decide on the very life of a spiritual organization. Where real authority has passed from the individual church member to the ministers and a denominational organization, it is not surprising that membership can be gained by mere profession of faith and retained regardless of conduct in society. An implication of this is that if the modern Roman Catholic Church is going to give real financial and administrative authority to its laymen it will inevitably start raising its standards of membership.

If strictness of membership criteria varies directly with the authority of the members, we also need to add that the length of training required for ordained ministers will tend to vary with the authority given to them. The Roman Catholic Church has insisted on at least seven years training, because so much power has been centered in the parish priest. In churches whose members can hire and fire their pastor by the votes of a church meeting, there is much more experimentation with untrained ministers. The Presbyterians usually compromise by limiting the congregation's choice to a seminary-trained, approved minister; but the congregation has no right to dismiss him except by the slow process of making his work so unsatisfying that he leaves voluntarily. More of this in our discussion of the ministry (Ch. XV).

A third observation is that discipline in the Christian church centers around the word excommunication. Full members take communion, and if they lose their right to the bread and wine they are outcasts from the society, and usually considered outcasts from God also. There was admittedly a time when prelates had so much power in civil matters that they could have offenders burned at the stake or tortured till they saw the ecclesiastical light. But such temporal power has happily not been the norm except in Europe. If the American doctrine of the separation of church and state had no other virtue than its prevention of churches' using magistrates to enforce faith and love, it would still be one of the greatest and most humane doctrines in all politics.

Excommunication implies that the privileges of church membership are so high that to be expelled is the ultimate tragedy.

In the Roman Church the terror of excommunication was that it automatically involved exclusion from heaven also. In the close brotherhoods of some Protestant groups exclusion from the bread and wine meant the censure of friends, the loss of sweet fellowship, the consciousness of being out of favor with God and man. Today when men neither fear hell nor long for heaven, and fellowship is more a bore than a delight, excommunication has withered into meaninglessness.

As we turn to baptism the path is thorny. The closest of Christian friends may flush with anger. Families have been divided. The controversies have filled weighty and bitter books. Virtually all Christians are agreed on the need for baptism, since Jesus Christ himself gave the example and commanded his disciples to baptize in all nations. Only Quakers and Salvationists have considered the rite unnecessary, and that for different reasons. George Fox had to remind us that religion is of the heart, an inner experience that is in no way tied to outward rituals. He made his point and struck greater blows for freedom of religion and freedom of the Spirit than any other Englishman. General Booth was more practical. The first thing was to rescue the drunks and knifers and harlots, and get them marching for Jesus Christ. To baptize or rebaptize would have angered the established churches: as it is "the Army" is still welcomed as a movement rather than a rival denomination by many Christians.

The mode of baptism need not detain us, since the age of baptism is obviously the real issue. Those who only baptize adults have nearly always required total immersion. The argument is centered on the meaning of the Greek verb *baptizo*, together with the symbolism of burial and resurrection (see Rom. 6:1-11). Infant baptisms are usually by sprinkling or pouring water on the head. The Greek Orthodox liturgy and the Anglican Book of Common Prayer still recognize that the infant should be put right under the water unless the parents can certify the child's health would be endangered by this. On the assumption that ministers are too clumsy or English babies less robust than in the good old days, this is rarely done. When challenged by their Baptist friends Anglicans will often counter by asking sarcastically why so few Baptists are called to evangelize the Eskimos or the Bedouins of the Sahara. When the argument can elicit no more than jokes about the quantity of water to be used, it is high time to return to the real issues, which relate to the candidates rather than to the manner.

If the church is the school of Christ, the crux of discussion is whether baptism is the sign of entering or the sign of attaining what the school stands for. Baptists, Mennonites, Pentecostalists, Brethren, Seventh Day Adventists, Jehovah's Witnesses, and many other smaller groups insist that baptism is after faith. Children cannot have conscious faith, so they obviously cannot qualify; and in fact no baptisms of children are specifically recorded in the New Testament. Baptism is a witness to God, to the congregation, and to himself that the candidate has accepted the offer of salvation and received eternal life by faith in Jesus Christ.

Churches that baptize infants do so as a sign of enrollment in the school of Christ. The best English schools have crests with a motto on the cap or blazer, which is proudly worn from the day the child is admitted. The crest gives no guarantee that the boy has ever attended a class, let alone learned what the motto stands for, but even the fact of being accepted in the school has great honor, privilege, and hope of attainment. Enrollment says more about the parents' faith than the child's own efforts, but ultimate success will also depend on his cooperation. So with baptism. None is too young to be enrolled, since Jesus Christ welcomed little children, and learning begins from the mother's first prayer over the cradle. At the same time none is too old, so that in some cases an old man may decide because of his own faith to join the "school." Mostly it is the parents' faith that causes the process of learning to begin, but the meaning of baptism is incomplete without acceptance and faith on the part of the growing child.[1]

This means that churches that practice infant baptism must have a ceremony corresponding to believers' baptism when

---

[1] For further discussion, see Pierre Marcel, *The Biblical Doctrine of Infant Baptism.*

the grown child is ready to take for himself what his parents have introduced him to. Usually this is connected with taking of the bread and wine in the communion service. Anglicans and Presbyterians call it confirmation, Roman Catholics make much of the first communion, others extend the right hand of fellowship or accept into membership. Churches that practice believers' baptism may or may not have another ceremony after baptism for admission into a particular local church membership. The act of admission to voting privileges in a local congregation is in any case distinct from adult baptism, or baptism plus confirmation, which is usually regarded as the sign of admission into the universal church. Thus most Baptist churches accept an individual who has expressed his faith by believers' baptism in another denomination, and Anglicans who have been confirmed can take communion in any Anglican church throughout the world, but this does not give automatic voting rights in the local Baptist church or the Anglican parish council, for which other conditions are laid down. If the Roman Catholic Church is going to develop a concept of local church membership with voting powers in a parish council, then they will also require a stronger sign of acceptance into local membership.

In churches with a Calvinistic tradition, much is made of baptism as the New Testament equivalent of circumcision. Circumcision is a sign of God's covenant with man. Abraham first had saving faith and received the sign as an adult, but then his children were to be circumcised on the eighth day. The sign was quickly misunderstood. Moses and the prophets had to keep reminding the people that outward circumcision was useless without inner heart circumcision (Deut. 10:16; 30:6; Jer. 4:4).

Just as circumcision was constantly misused and misunderstood, so baptism has often appeared more of a hindrance to true faith than a help. It is essential that if infants are baptized the parents are reminded of their responsibility to teach the Bible, and the children brought to make that faith personal for themselves. Most theologians are now agreed on the need for personal faith to make the meaning of baptism complete or fully effective. Whether the children of faithful parents should be baptized with a view to faith or after conscious faith is still being discussed. Those who baptize children have many centuries of history on their side, but the churches that baptize only believing adults have grown far more rapidly in the past one hundred years. Certainly adult believers' baptism makes the need for personal decision much more vivid, and it has usually produced a far more vigorous membership than in the churches that baptize infants. It remains to be seen whether the latter can add the stress on faith and active membership after baptism that has characterized the former.

What about the unbaptized? Here also theologians have come much closer to agreement. The thief on the cross was obviously not handicapped because there was no time for baptism before his death. We are saved by faith, not by the sign of faith. After enrollment, a soldier or policeman will normally wear the uniform, but it is certainly conceivable that in special cases there may be ununiformed soldiers or policemen. There are also the deserters, and there may be those who walk around the barracks in uniform but have no part or lot with the genuine, and may in fact be there for vicious motives. Baptism is for every Christian, but it neither guarantees, nor does its absence necessarily exclude, a share in the true church of God.

So much for visible signs. We now turn to the vital, organic, inner life of the church.

Six

Fruit and Gifts

The mystery of the church is mirrored by the mystery of the human body, and twentieth-century medical science has enriched the comparison. "We are to grow up in every way into him who is the head, into Christ, from whom the whole body, joined and knit together by every joint with which it is supplied, when each part is working properly, makes bodily growth and upbuilds itself in love" (Eph. 4:15f.).

Everyone reading this book came originally from one fertilized cell. That cell grew and divided, and the two split into four, and the four into eight; and now we understand each other because our millions of cells formed us into what we are. The mystery is that the cells did not merely multiply, or we would have become a great lump of tapioca pudding. There had to be diversity. But how awesome were the millions of decisions without which we would have become monsters. Why did the eye cells decide to be retina, or automatic lens, or optic nerve? How did each bone know its shape and angles? And how does every one of our billion cells agree to cooperate in fighting sickness or a serious accident? And when did the brain cells first invent computers? Scientists expect to explain all this by means of DNA codes, and we will applaud the Ph.D.'s and Nobel prizes that are earned in the process. The greatest of them will, however, retain a sense of awe and mystery, because having described everything they will know that reality has still eluded them. When a rose is explained by science, the lover of flowers shakes his head and says, "They have described what remains after a rose is dismembered and dead."

Certain basic facts are apparent. Cells build up the body under the influence of something that may be called the life force. When death occurs, or cells are separated from the life force, disintegration begins. In Paul's illustration of the church as the body of Christ, the Holy Spirit corresponds to this life force. He creates, energizes, unites, and directs each cell, and apart from him we are dead.

Every cell has some things in common, and something that makes it different. The millions of cells of one body have identical chromosomes, and every member of the body of Christ is characterized by the family likeness. We should be recognizable by the fruit of the Spirit, love that has an eightfold spectrum of joy, peace, patience, kindness, goodness, faithfulness, gentleness, and self-control (Gal. 5:22; cf. I Cor. 13:4-7). Innumerable devotional books have expounded this Christlike pattern and noted its rarity among those who profess it.

Our task here is to concentrate on diversity. Every cell has that inner compulsion that should make it different from all others, a "gift" that enables it to do its work in the right place at the right time in the body. If the fruit of the Spirit makes a Christian grow into the family likeness, the gifts of the Spirit will make him mysteriously different. Just as cells can be grouped by function into bone cells, liver cells, muscle cells, epidermis cells, and so on, so Christians vary according to their function in the body of Christ.

Paul makes lists of these functions in three different epistles. Though scholars will disagree about their exact classification, we may group them roughly as follows:

GIFTS OF THE SPIRIT (*CHARISMATA*)

Ephesians 4:11, 12	Romans 12:6-8	I Corinthians 12:28-30
APOSTLES		APOSTLES
PROPHETS	PROPHECY	PROPHETS

EVANGELISTS		
PASTORS	EXHORTERS	
TEACHERS	TEACHER	TEACHERS
	SERVICE	HELPERS
	CONTRIBUTOR	
	RULER[1]	ADMINISTRATORS
	DOER OF MERCY	
		MIRACLE
		WORKERS
		HEALING GIFTS
		TONGUES
		INTERPRETERS

Evidently Paul has not arranged these gifts in any exact order. The five mentioned in Ephesians are those usually associated with what we have called the ordained ministry (though in the New Testament there is no such distinction). Other gifts are listed in an earlier section of I Corinthians 12. It is tempting to fit wisdom and knowledge *(gnosis)* and faith with those in the chart, but we must recognize that there may not be any correspondence; and there could be discussion as to whether eight, twelve, or sixteen, or twenty different gifts existed in the early church. The important thing is to recognize the fact that there were spiritual gifts among Christians, and that in our modern church situations we have largely obscured these distinctions. If the church is to be renewed to do its task in the world today we need Christians who are gifted with a variety of gifts in every local church. Little progress can be made as long as we hold the strange idea that a minister can be hired who exercises all the gifts, while the laity listen to him, pay him, and get involved in what he chooses to organize.

Before turning to a tentative study of what these gifts are, and how they may be restored to full use in our churches, certain qualifications must be made. First, we must stress that

---

[1] The first meaning of the Greek verb *proistemi* is "to be at the head, to rule, to direct." The RSV has wrongly taken the second meaning, "to be concerned, to give aid," which duplicates the previous gift. See under *proistemi* in W. F. Arndt and F. W. Gingrich, *A Greek-English Lexicon of the New Testament* (Chicago: University of Chicago, 1957).

these are gifts of the Holy Spirit. They are not thought up or produced or chosen by men. "All these are inspired by one and the same Spirit, who apportions to each one individually as he wills" (I Cor. 12:11). Every Christian who is indwelt and filled by the Holy Spirit will have one or more of these gifts, which he is responsible to discover, develop, and exercise. He has no right to pick and choose: these are "gifts."

Second, we can infer from the New Testament that some men, like Paul, had several of these gifts, while others humbly gave themselves to exercising one. Paul certainly does not expect all Christians to have all the gifts (I Cor. 12:29f.). Most of us are one-talent people, some are gifted with two, and it is only occasionally that there is a great Christian leader with five talents. Whether we have five, or two, or one, the reward is the same, provided we use our talents to the full.

Third, Paul indicated that the various gifts of the Spirit are no proof of salvation. His great chapter on love, which follows the chapter on gifts, shows that it is possible to speak in tongues, to preach as a prophet, to understand all biblical truth, to work faith-miracles, and to sacrifice everything in generous giving to the poor, and yet be nothing (I Cor. 13: 1-3). Jesus taught the same truth when he said, "On that day many will say to me, 'Lord, Lord, did we not prophesy in your name, and cast out demons in your name, and do many mighty works in your name?' And then will I declare to them, 'I never knew you; depart from me, you evildoers' " (Matt. 7:22f.). The fact is that hypocrites can duplicate all the gifts, whether prophecy, or evangelism, works of mercy, tongues, or self-giving service. Every Christian should have one or more spiritual gifts, but no gift is a proof of righteousness with God. The spectrum of qualities that springs from love of God and love for man — the fruit of the Spirit — *this* is reliable evidence; and without love no man is anything.

One more question should be answered before we turn to a detailed study of the gifts. How do Christians find out what gifts they have? It is difficult to say much about this apart from the context of a functioning local church in which there is room for all the gifts to appear. In such a fellowship men and women have the opportunity to exercise themselves in many directions. A group of boys who gather to play football will gradually arrange themselves into the team positions where each can make the best contribution. Alone it would be impossible to determine one's gifts. The fact is that gifts are better recognized by others than by oneself. When others encourage someone to exercise his gift, he has some assurance that he has a contribution to make, and he will practice and develop in that direction.

The frustration of gifts that have been repressed has broken out into a large number of new Protestant movements, which have tended to organize churches according to individuals' gifts. Some consist of members who delight in deep Bible study or in evangelistic activities. Others gather those with the gift of tongues. Some churches devote themselves to works of mercy or intensive committee administration. The Roman Catholic Church has tried to restrict the exercise of the gifts to a highly disciplined full-time priesthood; other churches speak much of the priesthood of all believers and the ministry of the laity, but they are horrified if the gifts ever threaten to infringe the prerogatives of the professional association. No wonder laymen have found it hard to discover their gifts when faced with the choice of a one-sided but enthusiastic denomination or a church where only the ordained ministry is expected to have any gifts at all.

Any discussion with a group of Christian "laymen" will indicate that many of our best men feel that their gifts are unrecognized and repressed. This frustration keeps erupting into new movements organized by laymen where they can channel their energies. Against this fragmentation we must somehow recover the concept of the body of Christ. In *every* congregation *every* gift of the Spirit should be encouraged, and *every* member should find his place. The problems of testing the gifts, rejecting what is spurious, controlling misguided enthusiasm, and maintaining the unity of the Spirit in the bond of peace,[2] all these are tremendous. The risk of mistakes

---

[2] Eph. 4:3. Paul's stress on unity comes wherever he mentions the variety of gifts: Eph. 4:3-12, Rom. 12:3-8, I Cor. 12:4-26.

and deviations is serious, but surely it would be better than the certainty of frustrated ineffectiveness.

Seven

Tongues and Interpretation

It is tempting to avoid discussing the controversial until the acceptable has been accepted, but our consideration here cannot escape the controversial; tongue-speaking is needed to explain the other gifts. In any case many readers will begin with this chapter to form an opinion about the book as a whole. For or against tongue-speaking, opinions are strong, and the whole church is discussing a rediscovery of the doctrine of the Holy Spirit, in which the understanding of "tongues" is central. I shall begin with two obvious facts that will soon indicate the direction of my prejudice.

The Corinthian Church spoke in tongues as a regular practice, and Paul certainly did not discourage them (I Cor. 14; esp. v. 39). There are at least three other passages in the New Testament where tongues are mentioned, usually in connection with receiving the Holy Spirit.[1]

Secondly, speaking in tongues as part of regular church meetings, as opposed to private experiences that may have been more common, seems to have died out until this century.[2]

---

[1] Acts 2:4 (Jerusalem); 10:45-47 (Caesarea); 19:2-6 (Ephesus); Mark 16:17 (in the ending of Mark not accepted as genuine by most scholars).

[2] The year 1906 is usually counted as the date of the beginning of the Pentecostal movement. The first officially organized Pentecostal denomination was the Elim Four Square Gospel Alliance in 1915.

There are three explanations for this eclipse. One is that tongue-speaking is a psychological by-product of religious excitement with similar manifestations in Greek religion, the voodoo sects of Haiti, and certain oriental cults. Or we can say that this was the miraculous unrepeatable sign of the inauguration of the New Testament era, so that all subsequent manifestations are spurious. Those who have experienced speaking in tongues usually assume that just as it took fifteen centuries — until the time of Reformation — to rediscover justification by faith, so it has taken nineteen centuries to rediscover the power of the Holy Spirit. Peripheral; superseded; rediscovered — these are the three options. If we hold to the "rediscovered" view, we can say either that it is an essential experience for all Spirit-filled Christians, or that it is a possible manifestation for those who have this gift. What follows is based on the latter view. I am convinced that there have been and there are genuine manifestations of this gift of the Holy Spirit, but I am equally convinced that there are men and women who are filled with the Holy Spirit without this particular gift. I hope I can remain on the happiest of Christian terms with those who hold the other views.

If tongue-speaking is a gift of the Spirit with genuine manifestations in our day, as well as much spurious excitement, what exactly is its nature? Nineteen hundred years before modern psychology Paul made an important distinction between conscious mental activity and the deeper level of the spirit. He stated that it is possible to use one's vocal cords to pray, sing, or speak, under the direct control of the subconscious as well as mediated through the thinking mind. "If I pray in a tongue, my spirit prays but my mind is unfruitful (inactive). What am I to do? I will pray with the spirit and I will pray with the mind also; I will sing with the spirit and I will sing with the mind also. . . . In Church I would rather speak five words with my mind, in order to instruct others, than ten thousand words in a tongue" (I Cor. 14:14f., 19). The experience of singing without using one's conscious mind is common. Most Christians have experienced times of prayer when they know they have communicated with God from the deepest level of their being, but used no articulate words.

Speaking in tongues can be viewed as a similar activity, in which the subconscious communicates to others directly through the vocal cords without using the mind to construct sounds, words, and grammatical sentences.

This explains why the experience of speaking in tongues is so often connected with an outpouring of spiritual life. Men and women are so impressed with this new experience that they are unable to express it in words. In a sympathetic environment they may feel free to use their vocal cords to communicate what they now know with the assurance that others can understand. Their tongue communicates but not according to usual phonetic rules. We can also see why those who have been used to a well-ordered, carefully thought-out devotional life find it so hard to disengage their conscious minds to seek the experience of "tongues." Some who have sought to speak in tongues have through this discovered that their spiritual experience was cold and calculated; and in letting go of themselves they have really found God. Others with a genuine experience of God have looked for the something extra that "tongues" might give them, and not finding it have been unnecessarily frustrated. The essential experience, which may or may not be accompanied by "tongues," is to find oneself loving God with all one's heart; and this should lead to loving him with all one's mind as well. If seeking for "tongues" brings one to seeking to know God in this way, then the seeking has ended in the right direction. If on the other hand one who already loves God with all his heart and all his mind is then persuaded that he needs to look for an experience we should not be surprised if unhealthy results are produced, whether or not he speaks in "tongues."

We need to distinguish the experience of speaking in "tongues" that are incomprehensible, which therefore need interpretation, and the unique experience of Pentecost. There is no doubt that on that occasion the hearers were able to understand the Galilean disciples without distortion of dialect or even of native language. There was a direct communication from heart to heart without any language problem. That this occurs from time to time with particular individuals even today seems probable. There is a growing body of literature on

ESP, the phenomenon of extrasensory perception. Some people have an astonishing power of knowing directly without the use of spoken words, or through spoken words in a quite unknown language. It seems that simple and so-called primitive people have often retained this direct avenue of knowledge better than our city dwellers. There may have been a time when men communicated from heart to heart much more than we do now.

We assume that grammatical and syntactical language is necessary for conveying information, but this belief arises only because that is the way we happen to communicate now. Marshall McLuhan has helped us to see the change from tribal to mechanical man that took place as a result of printing. Now he predicts the emergence of a new universal tribal consciousness through the extensions of man's mind made possible by electronics.[3] We can visualize a similar change in humanity long ago at the time when syntactical language first began. Before that, men may have communicated more directly without language distortion. The dividing effect of language may be indicated by the account of the tower of Babel (Gen. 11), when men began to go apart because they could no longer understand each other.

The day of Pentecost was a reversal of the curse of Babel. Again for a brief period men understood each other: they had a foretaste of the reunified humanity that the Messiah was beginning to inaugurate. It is not surprising that this type of direct communication in "tongues" was made possible by God on Pentecost, when the disciples first knew at the deepest level who Jesus was, and the hearers were gathered from every nation for the very purpose of attending what might be called the preview of the declaration of the gospel throughout the world.

Some will object that we have now made "tongues" into something ordinary and common, but this is also the case with all the other gifts of the Spirit. Christianity is superbly ordinary. The only difference is that ordinary activities are shot

---

[3] Marshall McLuhan, *The Gutenberg Galaxy* and *Understanding Media*.

through with loving God with all one's heart and one's neighbor as oneself. Without that love "tongues" are valueless. Jesus Christ will say "I never knew you" to many who preach in his name, cast out demons, and do other mighty works, so we can hardly expect "tongues" to be a better substitute than these for doing the will of God. Paul accepts the validity of "tongues" plus *agape*-love, but without the first and great commandment man is nothing but noise and a clanging (Matt. 7: 22f.; I Cor. 13:1). Evidently it is possible to speak in tongues and be lost. If an ungodly man speaks in tongues, his communication is Satanic. "Out of the abundance of the heart the mouth speaks." The tongue as a member and "tongues" as a gift are both ordinary and neutral; it is man's heart and the love of God that make the difference.

This may explain why there are recurring reports of the phenomena of "tongues" in other religions. Tibetan monks are said to quote from Shakespeare and use the profanity of drunken English sailors in the excitement of their ritual dances. Travelers describe similar outpourings from the subconscious among the voodoo sects of Tahiti, the dervishes of the Moslem world, and various animistic tribes. These reports all lack scientific documentation, and they may be largely exaggerated second-hand tales, but there is no possible theological reason for surprise if "tongues" and prophecy are found in other circles. Psychologists are only beginning to dip their toes in the vast seas of extrasensory perception and the group unconscious. Whether or not "tongues" will be satisfactorily explained as an ordinary psychological phenomenon, the New Testament clearly warns us against either accepting it as a proof of godliness in itself or opposing it as an evil to be rejected.

Let us imagine a twentieth-century situation where a group of people have suddenly come to know God in a vital way, and some have expressed this experience in "tongues." What advice would Paul give to them? First of all he is concerned that they learn to articulate their heart experience in understandable words. "Therefore he who speaks in a tongue should pray for the power to interpret" (I Cor. 14:13). He uses the illustration of three musical instruments. The beginner will make noises, but this should lead on to playing a tune or sounding a trumpet call. "If even lifeless instruments, such as the flute, or the harp, do not give distinct notes, how will any one know what is played? And if the bugle gives an indistinct sound, who will get ready for the battle? So with yourselves; if you in a tongue utter speech that is not intelligible, how will any one know what is said?" (I Cor. 14:7-9).

Evidently Paul would expect every speaker in tongues to go on to prophecy. "He who speaks in a tongue edifies himself, but he who prophesies edifies the church. Now I want you (or I am glad if you) all to speak in tongues, but even more to prophesy. He who prophesies is greater than he who speaks in tongues, unless someone interprets, so that the church may be edified" (I Cor. 14:4f.).

Secondly, Paul would bring the use of tongues under control. Obviously there must be room for the one who has not yet learned to articulate his heart experience in grammatical sentences. Tongues should not be forbidden, but there needs to be someone in the group with the gift of interpretation, otherwise they should keep quiet (I Cor. 14:28). The gift of interpretation enables a more experienced Christian to discern what the speaker in tongues is trying to say, and to put this into intelligible language. The interpreter knows grammatical language, but also understands the "prelanguage" of direct communication. In addition to requiring an interpreter for any speaking in tongues, Paul limits such participation to "two or at the most three" in one meeting; and this should not be a simultaneous pouring out of "tongues" but "each in turn" (I Cor. 14:27). Most of the meeting will be taken up with singing, reading of Scripture, and the expounding of the prophets and teachers. (Evidently Paul is not speaking of a formal meeting for public worship, but a small gathering where most of the group takes part.)

The third emphasis that Paul would bring is the encouragement of all to develop their gifts and to seek "the higher gifts" (I Cor. 12:31). Every Christian should use whatever gift he has. "Having gifts that differ according to the grace given to us, let us use them" (Rom. 12:6). The gift of tongues will normally develop into a gift of prophecy. Other incipient gifts will appear, and these should be encouraged. The gifts of teaching and eldership will probably take much longer to develop. Exercising mercy in an effective way is not a gift that can appear fully formed the first day. This is why "tongues" is so prominent as an immediate gift. Other gifts take time, but any Christian with the gift of "tongues" can express himself immediately. We should expect most of those with this immediate gift to move on to prophecy, which is discussed in the next chapter.

So far we have concentrated on "tongues" as a gift of the Spirit. Like teaching, evangelism, works of mercy, and the like, it is a specialist contribution to the life of the church. In this it needs to be distinguished from "tongues" in private devotion. As we saw earlier in the chapter the experience of direct communication by the Spirit through the subconscious to the conscious mind, but bypassing the reasoning intellect, is probably more common than we imagine. There are many who have found this type of prayer experience very helpful, and they often use the word "tongues" to describe it. Others prefer to confine the term to public exercise of the gift in a church meeting. Rather than argue about the definition, we ought to understand the experience. To insist that both in public and in private a Christian has no right to communicate unless he uses "normal" language is unreasonable. In a public meeting the use of "tongues" must be ordered and strictly controlled to avoid confusion. In private the bypassing of the reasoning intelligence in some form of "tongue" would probably be a help to many who still find it hard to pray unless they find the right word.

Eight

Prophets and Prophetesses

The contemporary church is deeply concerned about having a prophetic voice. The usual method for accommodating this concern is to appoint a committee at every conference to draft resolutions about items of social injustice. These resolutions are duly passed by assemblies, and then politicians are lobbied by the more persistent churchmen. If democratic procedures fail we have learned from Mahatma Gandhi how to organize marches and nonviolent demonstrations. The ecclesiastical "doves" are shocked at these undignified proceedings. The ecclesiastical "hawks" suggest that it is time to use holy violence to shake the entrenched bourgeois status quo. In any case the world is singularly unimpressed. God's way used to be to appoint a Nathan to remind David about Bathsheba's husband (II Sam. 12:1-15), an Elijah to speak about the matter of Naboth's vineyard (I Kings 21:17-29), an Amos to denounce the fat kine of Bashan who made their husbands oppress the poor so that they could sleep on beds of ivory, overeat, and spend a fortune on beauty ointments (Amos 4:1; 6:4-6). It was John the Baptist's preaching, not nicely worded resolutions in the Sanhedrin, that prepared a people to hear their God.

Where did these Old Testament prophets come from? How were such giants produced? Obviously they did not come fully formed from nowhere. Like Jesus they grew up in their home town. They spent more time than the ordinary with the creator. Having conversed with God, they rebuked one of the local landlords or the man who allowed his parents to starve or the farmer who hired laborers and paid their wages at his own convenience. The community relied on prophets to speak bluntly without fear of man wherever there was injustice. Gradually the man of God became known in widening circles by honest and true citizens across the land. The dishonest, the corrupt, the exploiters, the sex-grabbers, the domineering would hate them. When God spoke it was impossible to be indifferent. Peasants, nobles, priests, magistrates, and even the other prophets, high and low, all had to decide for God and his righteousness, or the voice had to be silenced. This is why Nathan could walk in to the king, tell a parable, and point the finger to say, "Thou art the man." No official, landlord, or merchant could escape the haunting fear that a recognized prophet might walk in and deliver a public rebuke. If the church today could produce such men, I suspect their voice would carry further than any pale resolutions.

The nearest equivalent to this today is the courageous newspaper editor or the radio commentator who is big enough to speak out. For the most part such men are concerned with being interesting, objective, and accurate, all punctuated with an occasional burst of righteous indignation if such is in line with public opinion. Once in a decade an editor becomes prophetic. Tycoons, racketeers, and crooks in political clothing tremble at his words. A city is saved from corruption, a public wrong is dramatically righted, only because one man was willing to insist on truth regardless of personal considerations. Perhaps more Christians could take time to be men of God, to look with God at history and society, and then write and speak from the housetops.

The problem is that all the great churches and even the most biblical of evangelical Protestants have agreed that prophets died out in the apostolic age. It would be very inconvenient for theologians and for the establishment if prophets were to appear again in our churches. Who would control them? The usual theory is that the message of all the New Testament prophets was distilled into our canon; and with the book of Revelation to take us to the end of time, no further word from God is to be expected. By definition all self-styled prophets must be cranks, although it is nice to use the term for the occasional scholar who rises above the academic requirements to say something interesting.

The contradiction between a completed canon of Scripture and a continuing line of prophets is unnecessary. At every stage the written Word of God has needed prophets to apply it to men's hearts in concrete situations. The test of a true prophet like Isaiah, Jeremiah, or Ezekiel was that he spoke according to God's law and never in contradiction to it (Deut. 13:1-5). For eighteen centuries Christians of all denominations have agreed that the written word of God is complete with the New Testament canon. I have no intention of denying this simple foundation of all Christendom. I do contend that prophets were taken for granted as an essential part of the New Testament church, that they continued to perform a vital function in the first half of the second century, and that they are needed desperately if the church is to be more than the worn-out record of a dead God in our modern world.

Before going further we should define carefully just what we mean. The issue is confused by the phenomenon of predictive prophecy, which the Modernists on the one hand deny as unscientific and the Fundamentalists on the other hand make the norm of prophetic function. The Modernist argument is simple. The future has not happened and man is free to make it what he wills. Therefore, prediction, as opposed to mere insight into the signs of the times, is scientifically impossible. I remember hearing a learned professor explain the rule of thumb for Old Testament exegesis: "If the prophecy is fulfilled in history, date it after the event." This method makes possible, for example, the delineation and numbering of the various Isaiahs according to the historical periods that obviously appear in the book.

The Modernist logic is unanswerable if we accept the premise that God is in time. If, however, we consider with Einstein that this universe is a limited space-time continuum, that God being eternal cannot be limited in time, and that he has in fact made space-time as an essential part of his creation, then the argument does not follow. It a prophet meets with God and looks at space-time as God sees, he will be able to look at and describe other parts of space-time. At face value, this is exactly what the prophetic books seem to do. They are a series of disjointed descriptions of vivid scenes at various points in the space-time continuum. Isaiah, for example, in chapter 53 sees the cosmic event of the death of the Son of God on the cross. He also saw other periods of history, such as the exile and restoration, as well as the events of his own century. If we draw a semi-circle representing time, and put God at the center, then we can visualize the prophet leaving his own spot on the time circle, going to the center and out again along another radius to see or be a seer[1] of another segment of space-time.

Whereas the Modernist's problem is that he cannot believe that the prophet can *fore*tell as well as *forth*tell, the Fundamentalist is too interested in the details of his prophetic charts to note the importance of social righteousness in God's plan for men and nations. It is true that God demonstrates his control of history by giving long-term and short-term prophecies of every major event in Scripture. The whole argument of Isaiah 41:21–48:16 is based on the fact that God had predicted the earth-shaking events of the seventh and sixth centuries B.C., while the idols had been dumbly silent. When the prophecies were fulfilled and Cyrus had completed his predicted appointment, Israel was to understand and be wise.[2] This line of apologetics is part and parcel of biblical history, but it is evident that predictive prophecy was only a by-product from the point of view of the prophet himself. Peter tells us that in fact the predictions were enigmatic when delivered (I Pet. 1:10-12). Most of what the prophets had to say concerned flesh and blood social situations, which were only too obvious to their hearers. Predictive prophecy was essential for God's historical revelation, but it is not essential to prophetic activity. Some of the New Testament prophets did give predictions, and we cannot

---

[1] A common Hebrew name for a prophet.
[2] Isaiah 41:22, 23, 26, 27; 42:9; 43:9-12; 44:7, 8; 45:21; 46:10, 11; 48:3-5, 14, 16 are all nonsensical unless God does in fact control history and can predict in advance what is to happen.

rule out the possibility of prediction today; but whether or not there is an element of prediction, the prophetic voice is essential for God's action in and through his people.

If we were again to have prophets in the twentieth-century church, what would they do, how would they be prepared, and how would the administrators fit them into the denominational budgets? Let us begin with the New Testament churches as a norm, and then ask ourselves how our present outlook could be adapted to think and act the way they did. We can begin with Paul's concise definition. "He who prophesies speaks to men for their upbuilding and encouragement and consolation" (I Cor. 14:3). This is said in the context of speaking to an organized Christian congregation. Immediately many ministers will say, "Oh, if that's what you mean by prophecy, of course I agree with you. That's exactly what I try to do every Sunday. I build them up in the faith, I exhort them to Christian living, and I console those who are downhearted. I guess that makes me a prophet." There are men of God in our pulpits who try to discover what God is saying to his people. They do build up, encourage, and console. But are they in fact functioning as prophets in the way Paul meant it? Undoubtedly many ministers in our various denominations, and laymen too, have a prophetic gift and they could function as prophets in the New Testament sense, but there seems to be something lacking.

In the first place there is the question of time and concentration. The man who is hired to be a minister is expected to do many things. He has no time to wait on God. He is narrowed down to the pressing problems of one congregation, so that he is unable to see the movement of God and of evil in the world. He is expected to keep office hours and sit on numerous committees, until he comes to the point of assuming that he is paid to keep busy. He would be seriously misunderstood if he remained silent for a week and refused to see those who came to see him.[3] If there were prophets who had time to think and see as God sees, some of them would undoubtedly have something prophetic to say. They might meet the hunger of modern

---

[3] Compare, for example, Ezek. 3:15; 8:1; 11:1.

man, who desperately needs a word from God rather than a boring diet of hastily prepared exhortations. The problem is that our modern congregations do not, and probably cannot, allow their minister to be a prophet.

It is not just a question of a little word of building up and a few encouraging and consoling thoughts. The building up is lifting men and women out of the humdrum into the great movement of God in history. The encouragement of real *paraklesis*[4] is the application of the Holy Spirit, the Paraclete himself, to shake man to the very core and stand him up on his feet again to do exploits for God. Consolation is. God's fierce and loving answer to the very problems of existence and death that no man can answer. There *are* men of God who preach in this way, but they are too few; and the few need to be released for the whole people of God rather than building up a large single congregation while hundreds of others starve for a word from the Lord.

If lack of time is the first problem, the second is the lack of freedom to move; and this is largely a financial matter. Congregations will pay to have their own man of God if he can swell the attendance and the offerings. They will pay considerably less to send him as a missionary overseas. But to support a man of God with the freedom to be a prophet in the nation is unthinkable. The fact is that we have no equivalent of the first- and second-century prophets. Thomas M. Lindsay well described such men. "Those so endowed were in no sense office-bearers in any one Christian community; they were not elected to an office; they were not set apart by any ecclesiastical ceremony; the Word of God came to them, and they spoke the message that had sent them. They came and went as they pleased. They were not responsible to any society of Christians. The local church could only test them as they appeared, and could receive or reject their ministrations. The picture of these wandering preachers, men burdened by no cares of office, with no pastoral duties, coming suddenly into a Christian community, doing their work there and departing as suddenly, is a

---

[4] This is the New Testament Greek word for encouragement, but it includes much more than our "encouraging word."

vivid one in sub-apostolic literature."[5] Even if we approved of prophets in this sense, how would they live in our sprawling cities?

Lindsay notices the ministry of prophets in the early Christian congregations. We know that prophets moved in this way because they are mentioned in writings such as the *Didache*.[6] Is it too much to assume that they also performed a prophetic function in society? Or do we have to believe that whereas the Old Testament men of God spoke to kings and cities and nations, their New Testament equivalent confined their words to Christian ghettos? Certainly John the Baptist had no hesitation in rebuking Herod Antipas. Some of the great patristic preachers, among them Chrysostom and Ambrose, addressed their words to emperors and empresses. They remind us of the prophetic tradition, although the tendency to limit them to a particular church congregation was already evident. The case is not proved, but the evidence is sufficient for us at least to pray that God might of his mercy raise up some Hoseas, Amoses, Deborahs, and Habakkuks, to speak from God to our proud, sick world. Let each denomination and congregation and Christian decide how such men can eat and be warmed and pay their social security, so that they can give what the world so badly needs.

Spiritual concentration, prophetic preaching, mobility in the bloodstream of the body of Christ, discernment of the signs of the times, the rebuke of social wrongs, and the freedom to be a prophet without financial shackles — these are the marks of the gift of prophecy. God must call, the Holy Spirit must empower, but the church must recognize and make possible the exercise of the gift.

How do such men fit into our B.D.-level seminary training program? The answer is simple. They do not, they will not, and they should not. Nor do they fit into our present scheme of the ordained ministry, a matter to be discussed in Chapter XV.

What about the spurious prophets? We have had enough in

---

[5] Thomas M. Lindsay, *The Church and the Ministry in the Early Centuries,* pp. 72, 73.

[6] A.D. 100-130; for further information see *The Apostolic Fathers,* ed. J. B. Lightfoot.

our generation to bring the name of prophet into disrepute. As we saw in Chapter VI, Jesus warned us against false prophets, whom he has not sent. Many of these will be told, "I never knew you: depart from me, you evildoers" (Matt. 7:15, 22). Large numbers of false prophets are mentioned by the New Testament writers, and Christians are responsible for testing them. "Beloved, do not believe every spirit, but test the spirits to see whether they are of God; for many false prophets have gone out into the world" (II Pet. 2:1-3; I John 4:1-6). One of the problems with all the gifts of the Spirit is that whenever they are truly exercised ungodly men will begin to duplicate them. We should beware of the self-styled prophet. "By their fruits ye shall know them" is Christ's advice, and fruits do not appear overnight. Over a period of years a prophet will establish his right to be heard and the reliability of his word according to the written revelation of God and the good fruits of his preaching. We need to watch for the false, but as in all other cases the existence of counterfeits is no argument for denying oneself the genuine.

One final question. In his sermon on the day of Pentecost, Peter declared the prophecy of Joel was now fulfilled and that all God's people — men and women, young and old, free men and slaves — would prophesy. Every Christian is to exercise a prophetic function to his neighbor, in his job, in society. How do we square this with the fact that some specialists, the prophetic men who give themselves to waiting on God and studying history and the signs of the times, range widely across society to speak for God? The distinction is simple, as we shall see in the next chapter. Every Christian will exercise mercy when there is an obvious need that he can meet, but some Christians will give themselves entirely to the gift of mercy. So all true Christians are prophets, and they will on occasion speak prophetically to a neighbor, on a committee, or in society; but some men of God will give themselves much more exclusively to developing and using the prophetic gift imparted to them by the Holy Spirit for this purpose.

Nine

Mercy and Healing

Even if there were enough prophets there would still be physical
need. Should not every Christian be involved in social action?
Can one be right with God and ignore the poor, the sick, the
sordid slums? What about the starving millions a few hours'
jet flight away? Yet if we get too involved, our own family life
becomes impossible. We prefer to help through organizations
on a strictly limited liability basis. Then we read the terrifying
parable of the sheep and the goats: "As you did it not to one
of the least of these, you did it not to me." It is said that
Liberal churches have preached the social gospel most loudly,
while Evangelicals have emphasized the gospel, which admittedly has surprising social by-products. In any case most ordinary
Christians have a nagging feeling that they ought to be doing
more good, and their conscience is hardly salved by passing on
last year's fashions to the needy poor. Meanwhile it has become
obvious at both the local and international levels that it is the
do-gooders like Lady Bountiful who are most hated by the
objects of their charity.

To clarify the issues we must begin with Jesus' parable of the
Good Samaritan. We all agree that the bleeding man must be
bandaged and helped to the nearest inn. Regardless of personal
danger from the robbers, and in spite of the inconvenience, this
much we feel we ought to do. None of us will excuse the priest,

or prophet, or evangelist, or even the pagan who passes by on the other side. Most Christians would also agree that a contribution to the innkeeper to pay immediate expenses, since the man has been robbed, is fitting and commendable.

So far there is no problem. The real question is the degree and direction of further involvement. Immediately we are faced with many alternatives. We could found an organization and raise funds to help needy travelers. Or should travelers be protected by expanding the police force? Should I leave my business to take a medical course so I can give better treatment to the wounded? Or perhaps I should pursue a teaching career so that I could steer the next generation of youngsters away from banditry. Maybe it is a political matter, and if there were full employment there would be no need for robbers to rob. Should I then take up Keynesian economics or try for a position in local or national government? If, however, it is the heart of man that is the problem, then perhaps a Jericho Road mission — with a converted robber to speak to his own kind — is the most realistic answer. Other possibilities are community centers, adult education, rehabilitation of criminals in the jails, boys' clubs, or better qualified psychologists for family counseling. Any one of these and many other avenues of service would represent involvement in the social problem of highway robbers. A local congregation with a variety of spiritual gifts might well be able to touch the problem in all these directions through its members.

In this chapter we will concentrate on two spiritual gifts through which a church will be involved directly to touch the needy and the sick. The New Testament does not contrast social gospel and evangelical gospel. Every church is evangelical and every church has some gifted members meeting the needs of society.

Among a list of other gifts of the Spirit, Paul includes "acts of mercy," adding that the manner of this gift is to be "with cheerfulness" (Rom. 12:8). This is not the act of mercy that every Christian must do when he is faced with immediate need on the road to Jericho. It is a spiritual gift of the same order as the gifts of prophecy, teaching, administration, and shepherding. It is a function of the body of Christ that should be evidenced in every congregation through some of its members. This is the gift that made Florence Nightingale set the standards for nursing. It goes out to touch the lepers in countries where all others shy away from the unclean. It appears in the Salvation Army and in the children's and old people's homes where love triumphs over mere hygienic arrangements. It still goes to befriend those who have no friends, and even loves the ugly hearted who deserve to be friendless.

The gift of mercy may be found in government social services and privately organized good works, but unfortunately charity often takes on a nauseating coldness. The genuine gift of mercy never makes another feel small. It does not descend with condescension. It comes alongside with a friendly cheerfulness. *He who does acts of mercy with cheerfulness.* Rather than treat others in a patronizing way, it creates dignity, hope, and the will to live again. It rejoices when others become independent, stand on their own feet, feel the power of God pulsating in their veins, and then become concerned for others. Mercy creates human values among the apparently valueless. It can never consider any person as a useless chore, to be kept alive only because euthanasia is forbidden.

Obviously such mercy requires specialization, so it needs some Christians to give themselves to this particular gift. All Christians will demonstrate it on occasion, but those to whom the Holy Spirit divides the gift will make it their vocation. Unfortunately some church members who might develop this gift are told that preaching, teaching, or evangelistic activities are the only avenues of Christian service. In other churches those who should specialize in, say, administration, pastoral work, or creative writing feel guilty because they are not engaged more directly in works of mercy. A new sense of the whole body would free each Christian to fulfill his vocation, and Jesus Christ would do his works of mercy through those best fitted for this delicate operation.

If works of mercy are done mainly by means of hands and feet and listening ears, the gift of healing touches the sick through prayer. While a nurse is tending the patient's body, prayer for healing is reaching behind to the patient's mind and his subconscious. It is now a commonplace of medicine that faith is a tremendous healing agent, while the opposites of faith — resentment, anger, hate, anxiety, fear, despondency, and despair — are all killers. We must recognize that the ability to create healing faith is found among those who are not Christians and even among the unrighteous, who misuse their power for unworthy motives. There is, however, a Christian gift of healing. Like the other gifts it is very ordinary, a natural observable psychological phenomenon. When it is allied to the love of God, empowered by the Holy Spirit, and winged by prayer to the inner recesses of the heart, it has tremendous effect for good. "Pray for one another, that you may be healed. The prayer of a righteous man has great power in its effects" (Jas. 5:16).

In the verse before the one quoted, James indicates that healing is often connected with a confession of sin. Before faith can take hold, the hatred or jealousy or whatever it is may need to be recognized and cleansed. This may happen through preaching, Bible reading, or personal counseling, but it also occurs frequently when others are praying. The non-Christian counselor may be able to achieve a similar effect by suggesting that the sin is not sin, and so giving a release in another direction, but this kind of healing is often at the expense of creating indifference to moral values that may heal the body by damaging the person.

Prayer for healing combined with the ministry of the Word of God is far more common than appears on the surface. Many who are healed in a Christian community would be surprised at how others have prayed for them. Prayer for the sick is the privilege of all Christians, but there is a gift of healing that goes beyond this. "To another gifts of healing by the one Spirit" (I Cor. 12:9, 28). The man with a gift of healing knows how to pray the prayer of faith for others. He can discern and concentrate on the root of the trouble. Some have even had the experience of personal combat or absorbing the sickness of another in their own bodies. At this point the understanding of ordinary men fails. Those who have been helped by such prayer know that something miraculous has taken place. Those who exercise the gift know the hours and the agonizing in prayer. Others sense that their own prayer life is not in this direction, and they gladly call in the help of the man or woman with the gift of healing. Though the gift has been rediscovered in the church in this century, it is strange that so many are still suspicious, as if Jesus Christ and his apostles had never healed the sick.

At this point a warning is in order. Prayer for the sick or the gift of healing does not mean that everyone on whose behalf it is done will be healed. That some are miraculously healed I for one, as well as many others, take for granted. That many are not is equally evident. The whole New Testament generation and all generations since have died, and presumably there was prayer for each when they were sick. There are also sicknesses like Job's which are for other reasons. Some, like Paul's thorn in the flesh, are to enable a mighty man to keep small enough to be great. For many saints the time of sickness and death arrives when their work is done, while some little children may not need the experiences of life to perfect them. Death also comes to families, cities, and nations in times of judgment, and merciful prophets have been told to stop their prayer because God would not listen.

A true view of the gift of healing must go with a true understanding of death. For the atheist or agnostic, death must always be considered as the ultimate tragedy, since personality, significance, and hope are irrevocably terminated. From God's point of view physical death is never a tragedy, at whatever age and in whatever circumstances. This teaching is strong meat and strange to modern ears, but without it the prayer of faith for healing is doubly dangerous. To make healing a greater good than God's wisdom is idolatry. On the other hand, to deny that God intends to heal miraculously is a flat denial of his word.

The gift of healing is unlikely to appear fully formed. It is found among those who pray much, and in particular among those who care more for the wholeness of others than their own selves. It is developed by practice and sharpened in lonely vigils as life hangs in the balance. Like the evangelist and the apostle, the man who prays for healing needs the prayer help of others. The effect of prayer is multiplied when many agree together.

The ministry of healing also requires all the other gifts to support and correct it. The healer is particularly exposed to deviation from the truth. Without mercy to give the physical touch, prayer alone can seem cruel; and if all the church did were to heal bodies, would not its true end be utterly obscured? We should pray that God will give some with the gift of healing in every community. When they appear we must be careful to recognize them, welcome them, give them the fellowship of Christians with other gifts in the body of Christ. We should beware of the quacks and cranks and spiritual crooks who, like the false prophets, will also abound. And we need discerning caution not to throw out the gift of God with the counterfeits of Satan.

Ten

Evangelists and Teachers

Auto dealers are often caricatured as fast talking, high pressure, and probably dishonest. There are, however, salesmen with the gift of summing up the needs of the customer, judging the payments he can wisely afford, helping him to select the car suited to his family, and completing the sale with a minimum of fuss. The customer leaves satisfied, he recommends the dealer to his friends, and he can be expected to return for his next car in three years. Such salesmen may be rare, but obviously at its best the salesman's art is a public service. Most of us appreciate the man who can be helpful when we are trying to make up our minds. But when there is a shoddy product or a decision for which we are not ready, we resent the salesman with uncommon loathing.

So with the evangelist.[1] Given the fact that Jesus Christ is the pearl of great price, that we genuinely sense our need of him, and that we are ready to make a vital decision, the evangelist is a man who can help us. He is the salesman who helps us to see the issues, to choose, to commit ourselves. There are millions in the church today who are grateful for his help out of indecision. If, however, the evangelist's gospel is shoddy, his

---

[1] Ephesians 4:11 distinguishes this as a gift separate from teaching. Acts 21:8 mentions Philip as an evangelist, and Acts 8 illustrates his work in Samaria and with the Ethiopian.

methods uncouth, or our decision is forced, we do well to be angry.

The salesman differs from the engineer as the evangelist differs in temperament from the Bible scholar. Few engineers are good salesmen: they know too much, explain too much, and muddy the simplicity of decision. When a man needs a car he is not much helped by learned discourses on the internal combustion engine. The engineer is important in his place, but not in the selling situation. So the biblical scholar, the theologian, the expositor. They provide necessary functions in a sensible, well-taught church; but they rarely help the ordinary man who knows his sin, needs Jesus Christ, and longs for one who can direct him out of indecision into the peace of faith. The church must have salesmen, and the thousands who are grateful to Billy Graham for help in choosing life are sufficient answer to the wise who think that scholastic erudition is sufficient. The evangelist also illustrates the fact that men do not expect the church merely to provide mercy and healing and other good works. These things are necessary to accompany the Word of God, they may point to the truth, but apart from preaching they are a meaningless service to a meaningless world. It is as if the Ford Motor Company should provide a magnificent service organization without any means of selling the cars it proposes to service. A church that neglects the gift of evangelism is as near to disaster as a company that tries to do without its sales force on the assumption that good products sell themselves.

Having mentioned Billy Graham and the methods of mass evangelism, we need to counter two other reasonable objections. Like the salesman, the evangelist is tempted to press for results and to use the faster, slicker methods. These methods may put more people off than they help to true faith. This is a real danger, but at his best the salesman should be a man who genuinely cares for the customer: his motive is to satisfy rather than force. The evangelist also is human, and his chief temptation is to count heads, but temptation need not overcome a man of God. He can recognize the temptation and seek to guard against it. The fact of temptation and the occasional failure is in any case no argument against evangelism. If the church becomes too respectable to use her best salesmen, she cannot hope to fulfill her mission in the world.

This brings us to the other objection. If we are to have evangelists, why is it that we usually hear only the name of Billy Graham? One reason is that so few others have taken the time and efforts to excel in their art. When Paul names the spiritual gifts he exhorts us to give ourselves to our own gift (Rom. 12:6-8). The purpose of this study of the gifts in the body of Christ is to encourage us to specialize and seek excellence in our own function. Probably the chief reason for the lack of acceptable evangelists is that on the whole the church has not honored or encouraged this gift. Denominations are willing to pay for theologians, administrators, and ministers, but not for the evangelists who are most likely to make the church grow. It does seem indisputable from the evidence that churches that have stressed evangelism and evangelists have grown the fastest.

How are these "selling" evangelists going to be selected and trained? They are unlikely to benefit from existing requirements of a university degree followed by a three-year course of theological discipline. A theologian may also be an evangelist, but it is not because of his studies. Many evangelists are unlearned and ignorant men, as were Christ's disciples. The evangelist must have about the same level of education as his average listeners. His forte is to know the hearts of men and the language of the people, and to believe implicitly in what he has to offer. He will usually learn by doing, sometimes taking short refresher courses to keep up with the requirements of his work. He needs the supervision and encouragement of an experienced leader, and he will do better in a team than if left entirely to his own devices. If he becomes uncouth, or misrepresents the cause of Jesus Christ, there must be a way to correct him and if necessary dispense with his services.

After a period of apprenticeship in which a man has proved that he can present the claims of Jesus Christ with dignity and the power of the Holy Spirit so that men accept him as Lord, a man becomes an evangelist. It is now the church's responsibility to recognize him as such and to invite him to exercise his gift both in special meetings in the churches and in every place where he can be given a hearing in society. Every denomination should maintain a list of such approved men as well as give opportunities for younger men to develop this gift.

We must also recognize that the evangelist is likely to be an interdenominational man. His business is not to make labeled churchmen. He concentrates on helping men and women to believe in and accept Jesus Christ. After conversion the convert must be encouraged to choose a church where he feels at home, where he will be taught the duties of membership in that congregation. If, however, an evangelist is required to make Anglicans, or Baptists, or what-not, he himself will be frustrated, other denominations will accuse him of sheep stealing, and the poor sheep will wonder whether they are to decide about Jesus Christ or about the history and principles of a denominational system. If the most mature Christians find it hard to discern the right denomination for themselves, how unreasonable to force this decision at the point when the trembling soul is weighing the pearl of great price against the precious trivialities of this world.

By mentioning Billy Graham we may have given the impression that evangelists are by definition men who speak to great crowds. Jesus Christ told Peter and James and John that they would become fishers of men. We know that Peter was responsible for catching a large shoal of fish on the day of Pentecost. But fish can also be caught with a line and hook. We need the more elaborate arrangements for group evangelism and the use of the mass media, but we also need a large number of personal evangelists. Whitfield, D. L. Moody, and Billy Graham have excelled in large meetings, but thousands of unnamed Christians are catching men one by one. They too are evangelists, and the fish they catch may be inaccessible by any other means. The sales of insurance policies, race horses, financial empires, and the making of marriage agreements all need individual treatment that is unsuited to the sales floor, the television, or the marketplace. Every church needs experienced personal evangelists who know how to help their friends, neighbors, and even strangers put their faith in Jesus Christ. All Christians do this to some extent, but obviously there will be some who are especially gifted in this way; and these are the ones who should be encouraged to give themselves to this gift and leave some of the other work of the church to others.

If the analogy of "selling" has still left the reader with a bad image of high-pressure, result-counting sales, it may help to remind ourselves of what salesmanship and evangelism at its very best requires: genuine faith in the product, honesty, courtesy, a concern for the buyer's interests, a respect for him as a person who must be left free to make the ultimate decision, without embarrassment if he chooses not to buy. Men of this caliber may be rare, but they do exist, and it should be the Christian church that can produce them.

The title of this chapter is "Evangelists and Teachers." I have concentrated on the evangelistic gift because it is neglected in most of our respectable denominations. The place of the teacher in the church was brought back to prominence by the Reformation. Later the Sunday School movement of the nineteenth century encouraged a host of Christians to give themselves to teaching, though unfortunately it was often assumed that only the very young need teaching. Evidently there are still a large number of teen-agers, university students, married couples, and even senior citizens who would be open to Bible teaching if some took the time to learn their subject and present it in a modern, interesting way. The seminaries, theological colleges, and Bible schools, which are the new ecclesiastical feature of this century, have all helped to train teachers. As I have indicated, they may not be suitable for the nurture of prophets, evangelists, and the other gifts of the Spirit, but they have stressed an intensive study of the Bible, church history, other religions, and the various arts needed to teach others. On the whole, teaching is one gift that has not been neglected in Protestant churches.

In terms of numbers we can agree that the gift of teaching has been extended to a larger proportion of laymen. In competence our achievement is still mediocre, however. At secular schools and universities students are taught by experts in their own subjects, but when they come to learn in church they are subjected to intellectual baby talk. An acceptable quality of teaching cannot come from a life of frantic activity. No man can work forty or fifty hours at a job, fulfill his reasonable duties in society and at home, sit on countless committees, organize Boy Scout troops, men's groups, and camps and meetings for businessmen, and then say something worthwhile to a group of high school students on Sunday. The spiritual gift of teaching needs specialization, time for reading and hard study, several hours of class preparation, plus a contagious enthusiasm in communicating the Bible as the most thrilling book in the world. Most high school students are bored with the church because their precious time is wasted by Christians who say nothing worth listening to.

For the church at large we have very few specialists who can teach through the mass media. Books of Christian doctrine are produced and apparently bought, but one wonders how many of these are readable, let alone stimulating. Our best brains are siphoned off to seminaries where they are expected to write indigestible monographs for the half dozen other men in the world who can understand what they are talking about. In the past doctors of the church wrote so that literate men could understand, and Augustine, Aquinas, Luther, Calvin, and Wesley are much easier to read than our contemporaries. When a C. S. Lewis writes theology in his spare time and millions are fed by his books, our theologians still assume that he is shallow because he lacks footnotes, bibliographies, and thesis style. On the whole it is the Roman Catholic orders such as the Jesuits and Dominicans who have best freed their teachers for adequate specialization, though they also suffer from heaviness of presentation. The greatest battle is the battle of the mind, and it is won by words that are shot like bullets—smooth, sharp, powerful, and dead on target.

Kerygma and *didache*[2]—proclamation and instruction—the evangelist helping men to choose Christ and teachers disciplining them to think straight — these are two basic activities in the Acts of the Apostles and of every effective work of God today. Evangelism and teaching are the essential gifts for building the church, since without them no church is possible. The *bene esse*

---

[2] C. H. Dodd, *The Apostolic Preaching and Its Development.*

includes the gifts of healing, prophecy, administration, pastoral care, giving helps, and the like, but the irreducible *esse* is that men become Christians and learn in the school of Christ.

Eleven

Elders and Pastors

Government by elders is the oldest institution known to man. It has been basic to tribal organization in all ages and it is still found in all continents of the world. It is democracy at its best, since elders are from the people, accepted by the people, to govern for the people. It functions ideally when the group to be governed is small enough for everybody to know one another and when government is by word of mouth rather than by paper work. Once a nation or a city-state emerges, other forms of government, such as monarchy, oligarchy, republicanism, or a dictatorship take its place. According to the Bible the Jews had elders as a slave people in Egypt; their Palestinian towns were governed by elders; and eldership was a natural form of government for the synagogues that sprang up during the exile. Nationally the tribal eldership gave way to a senate or Sanhedrin during the Exodus. Except for a period of confusion when judges or chieftains were required, and another period when kings ruled, the Sanhedrin functioned continuously until the fall of Jerusalem in A.D. 70.[1]

In the transition from synagogues to Christian churches, which we noted in Chapter II, government by elders continued unchanged until the great persecutions forced the emergence of the bishop or chieftain system to give stronger leadership. As the church grew into a great national organization the emer-

---

[1] Exod. 4:29; Deut. 1:13; 19:12; I Kings 8:1; Ezek. 20:1.

gence of a senate or Sanhedrin almost came to fruition at Nicea and the other church councils. In fact with the popes the church became organized as a monarchy, except that its priest-kings, being celibate, did not continue from father to son. Since the Reformation, the Sanhedrin, in the form of a general assembly, reappeared among the Presbyterian churches.

In this chapter we are not concerned with eldership at the general assembly level, or even in presbyteries. We must concentrate on the elder as he functions to govern a local church congregation. There is no need for us to quibble about names, since a parish council, a session, a Baptist board of deacons, or a committee of management by any other name are all of the same species. As in the tribal eldership, they are from the people, and appointed or accepted by the people to govern for the people. The parish priest of the Middle Ages who ruled his parish without elders was the by-product of the feudal system. This may survive in feudal Spain, but in Roman Catholic countries where the winds of democracy have blown, a revival of the eldership in some form has become necessary. The only question that makes a difference at the local level is whether the priest or minister is the *esse* of the local church and it is he who brings the local eldership into being, or whether a local church can constitute itself with its own elders and then call one or more ministers for specialized functions. As we saw in Chapter II, a Jewish synagogue governed by elders may or may not decide to call a theologically trained rabbi for teaching functions. This question may continue to divide the so-called Catholic traditions from the Protestant, though in fact many Protestant ministers also function on the assumption that they are the *esse* that calls the parish council or session into being.

Having cleared the ground, we can now look more exactly at the elder as he is defined for us in the New Testament. He is a man who has the spiritual gift of government, which is listed with other gifts of the Spirit in both Romans 12 and I Corinthians 12.[2] When the apostles felt the time had come for the

---

[2] In I Cor. 12:28 *kuberneseis* means administrators. The RSV translation, "he who gives aid," in Rom. 12:8 is the second meaning of *proistamenos,* which should be translated "the one who rules, directs, or manages" as in AV and RV.

Jerusalem Church to have its own elders, they said, "Pick out from among you seven men of good repute, full of the Spirit and of wisdom, whom we may appoint to this duty."[3] Before returning home after their first missionary journey, Paul and Barnabas appointed elders in the churches that had grown up through their preaching (Acts 14:23; cf. I Thess. 4:12). When the Ephesian elders gathered at Miletus, Paul reminded them of their office. "Take heed to yourselves and to all the flock, in which the Holy Spirit has made you guardians [*episkopous,* 'overseers, superintendents'] to feed [*poimainein,* 'shepherd, tend, lead'] the church of God" (Acts 20:28). Paul also outlined for both Timothy and Titus the type of man that is required. The main qualifications are dignity, uprightness, and respect in the community, and evidence of ability to manage his own household and children (I Tim. 3:1-7; Titus 1:5-9). There is also a doctrinal qualification that requires a knowledge of the faith and the ability to correct those in error.

Evidently the qualities required in a Christian elder are very similar to those required in a typical tribal elder. It is not a question of being an old greybeard, but rather of having the respect of the community. Just as a tribal elder may be illiterate but aware of the traditions of the tribe and able to recognize corruptions that may be introduced, so knowledge of Christian doctrine is required in the elders of a church. In pioneer missionary situations there is no reason whatever to require elaborate educational qualifications. If illiterate tribal elders can remember vast amounts of tribal lore, Christian elders can equally well learn the New Testament accounts of the life of Jesus, the Acts of the Apostles, and basic Christian theology and ethics.

Some of the elders may also have other gifts of the Spirit. Stephen and Philip from the Jerusalem Church both engaged in preaching. Paul recommends that elders who preach and teach, in addition to acting as members of the church board, should

---

[3] Acts 6:3. As pointed out on page 16, these men are elders, not deacons. Seven was natural for a group of elders, since Josephus tells us that villages were governed by seven men (*Antiquities* iv. 8.14, 38), just as in India they are still governed by a group of five men *(panch).* The function of deacons is discussed in the next chapter.

be counted worthy of double honor. In the same passage he indicates that if an elder labors full time in a preaching ministry he should be supported (I Tim. 5:17, 18). In a village or tribal situation this might involve help in harvesting his crops, or giving grain and fruit to his family when he is on a preaching tour. This again is no different from what is done in an African or Asian community when a local man is sent on a mission to a government center or to another tribe.

Just as in the gift of teaching, there are many levels at which the gift of administration may be exercised. Basically there is a capacity for spiritual discernment and decision making. An elder should be able to recognize the gifts of others, encourage them to use them in the church, and to maintain the unity of the Spirit between the different gifts. Like James, the presiding elder of the Jerusalem Church, he should be able to bring a committee to a spiritual decision acceptable to all. At other levels the gift of administration is needed in many functions of the worldwide missionary enterprise. As with the other gifts, it needs to be developed, used, and sharpened to be an effective instrument in the life of the church. It does not depend on academic qualifications, or appointment from above, but on the freely given respect of those whom it serves.

If this is the function of local church eldership, it is evident that in the Roman Catholic, Greek Orthodox, and Anglican churches much confusion has been caused by the misuse of words. On the one hand the Greek word *episkopos,* which refers to an overseer, superintendent, foreman, supervisor, has been tied to *the* Bishop, the episcopate in the ecclesiastical sense. As Bishop J. B. Lightfoot has pointed out in his article on the Christian ministry, all elders were originally *episkopous* or bishops.[4] When, however, men came to positions of vast authority as *the* Bishop, and these became part of a hierarchy down from the pope through archbishops, bishops, and priests, then the function of local church elders was completely obscured. The low church Anglicans objected to the term priest in a sacrificial sacerdotal sense, and insisted that it was connected with the word *presbuteros,* or elder. This may be true, but it still does

---

[4] Dissertation I in *Saint Paul's Epistle to the Philippians.*

not help us to recover the true function of government by a local board of elders. Presbyterians do have elders in the New Testament sense, but the category of minister is retained as an automatic presiding elder, and communion services are not normally held without a properly ordained minister as opposed to a less properly ordained elder. Baptists have elders in the true sense, who can perform all that is needed for a local church without the need of an imported minister, but strangely they usually call their elders "deacons." It would simplify matters considerably if all Christians agreed that the group of persons who govern a local church should be called elders. When these elders call in a minister, pastor, teacher, or preacher to work in their community, he could be named according to the main work which he is expected to do. When representatives from a group of churches meet together for a conference, the one presiding could then be called bishop, chairman, president, superintendent, or moderator as interchangeable terms. How he was appointed and the tenure of his office, whether for one year, two years, or for life would still vary in different traditions. At least at the local level, which is where the vast majority of Christians need to function, the importance of local eldership could be understood and recovered.

What then of pastors? We are not thinking of the Pastor in the Baptist or Pentecostal sense, which is equivalent to the Minister among Presbyterians, and the Parish Priest among the higher churches.. We are considering a function in the body of Christ, a gift of the Spirit. It is the gift of those men and women who have a shepherd heart. They know how to weep with those that weep, and are truly happy with those that rejoice. They have a gift of sympathy, of *paraklesis* or coming alongside to encourage, to comfort, if necessary to correct. If we go to a Bible teacher to learn our theology and answer theological questions, we go to a man with a shepherd heart when we need pastoral help.

Unfortunately we have given the impression that *the* Minister, or *the* Pastor, or *the* Priest, is the only man suited for this. Some of them are, but others may be more suited to preaching or theological debate, and the sheep stubbornly refuse to open their hearts to them. Even if *the* Minister has a shepherd heart, and men and women come to him with their deep heart needs, the situation immediately gets out of hand because he is too busy. If people know he is available he will soon be swamped with counseling and then has no time for the healthy, since he is crushed with the problems of the spiritually sick. Every church needs several men and women who are pastors in this sense, and there is no reason why a big congregation should not have many. Some of the elders may also have pastoral gifts, but not necessarily so, and there will be others who can shepherd but cannot cope with committees. The fact is that hundreds and thousands of men and women in our churches have the pastoral gift, but they are never encouraged to exercise it. Too often they are told that they should either go to seminary and obtain a B.D. or they should sit quietly in their pews and listen.

How will these pastors be trained? As with the other gifts, all Christians will on occasion be called on to listen, to comfort, to feed the newborn lambs with milk. Some will find particular delight in this, and they will find their help is appreciated. "To him that hath shall be given." Having begun they do more: experienced pastors can teach them to listen better, to choose the right Scriptures to read by a bedside, to pray with understanding, to discern the heart troubles that need psychiatric or specialist care, to avoid the approach that is patronizing or causes unnecessary dependence instead of self-development. The pastor is essentially a local man. He or she knows the sheep by name and is available at short notice. If he is sent away for long periods of training or is continually absent for committee work or too busy preparing Sunday School lessons, the sheep will avoid bothering him and they will suffer and die alone.

When a church has those with an incipient gift of shepherding, the elders should recognize them. They can be encouraged to care for a special group of members, or to go out and look for the lost. If a minister is swamped with his own calls, he can delegate instead of trying to carry the burden alone. Those who are busy with individuals should not be pressed to teach in classes, sit on committees, or organize activities of various kinds. They should be freed to be the friends and shepherds that the community so desperately needs. At least they can listen, hear the heartbeat of the lost, and often even this will be appreciated. If they can bring a sheep back into the fold and feed a lamb until it can feed itself, they will share in the joys of heaven. Even if a church lacks great preachers, it can transform a community just by pastoral visits and shepherd care.

"And his gifts were that some should be apostles, some prophets, some evangelists, some pastors and teachers, for the equipment of the saints, for the work of ministry, for building up the body of Christ" (Eph. 4:11f.).

Twelve

Deacons and Helpers

Some of the great men of the Bible began as servants. Joshua was Moses' personal assistant before becoming a military captain, and he afterwards succeeded his master as leader of God's people. Elisha "arose and went after Elijah, and ministered to him" before assuming the prophet's mantle and a double portion of his spirit. Elisha in turn recruited Gehazi, who also might have made good, but he misused his place as secretary to obtain an unearned bonus of two talents of silver and two festal garments from Naaman the Syrian.

In the New Testament Mark was assistant to Paul and Barnabas on the first missionary journey, but he apparently felt homesick and returned to his mother in the middle of things. Happily Barnabas did not despair of him, and in spite of his failure Mark eventually had the honor of recording the Gospel Peter preached. On the second journey Paul took on Timothy in place of Mark, and he thrived under increasing responsibility in Paul's team. Eusebius reports the tradition that he became the first bishop of Ephesus.[1]

Evidently acting as assistant to a man of God is one of God's ways of training men for leadership. It is training by doing with a great man. Unfortunately twentieth-century Chris-

---

[1] This is included as a note at the end of the King James Version of II Timothy.

tians have shallowly assumed that only women are suited to be secretaries. This may be true if shorthand, typing, and answering the telephone are all that is required. In fact, the leaders of the most dynamic human enterprises use personal assistants; and most of these are men whose training as servants will be their best preparation for promotion. The army colonel has an adjutant, the general has a chief of staff, top administrators have assistants, and the most influential men in the diplomatic and civil services are called first secretaries. But the Christian church has allowed its professional training schools to suggest that a B.D. is all that is required for competence as a minister. Even more tragic is the pernicious idea that without a B.D. an otherwise outstanding man is unacceptable as a leader of God's people. This has denied Joshuas and Timothys the chance to give needed assistance for our most capable leaders, it has made it impossible to recruit for the ministry by direct call from other professions, and it has forced a larger number of inexperienced young men into responsibility for struggling and therefore difficult congregations. By all means let seminaries train to the best of their ability, but their graduates should compete with others who have been trained in a more practical way by working with a man of God.

We forget that seminary training as a requirement for ordination is a very new idea in the church of God. Theology as a special subject, the queen of the sciences, was a university discipline; it was only required as a preparation for academic work, not for the normal parish ministry. Seminaries were invented by the Council of Trent and ordered in all dioceses for the indoctrination of priests against the Lutheran heresy. Protestants trained their ministers through the universities or by the apprenticeship system for the best part of three centuries. The first Presbyterian seminary was in Pittsburgh (1794), followed by Princeton (1812) and Yale Divinity School (1822). The Anglicans had a college at Chichester in 1839, but it was not until well on in the twentieth century that graduation from a theological college was considered necessary. As Mark Gibbs and Ralph Morton note, "There have been a hundred Archbishops of Canterbury, but only three were trained in a theological college."[2]

The most effective training the church has had for the parish ministry was in Britain through the Anglican curacy system. Whatever his previous qualifications, the ordained man was required to become a deacon — a servant — to learn for two years under an experienced minister. Due to the shortage of men, the system has recently failed, since deacons are usually put in charge of daughter churches where they function as second-class ministers. American ordinands are expected to gain some experience as student pastors during their seminary training, after which they may become directors of education in a big church. This still means that there is no opportunity to be a real assistant and to learn under the responsibility of another. The point of the original Anglican system was that the curate or deacon was a genuine apprentice who learned by helping in all the work that his "master" had to do. Many of our best ministers today could well use a personal assistant or deacon, who in turn would learn more than he gave.

The original meaning of deacon or deaconess was just plainly this, a servant who helped a man of God or a church to function. Mark served Paul, Barnabas, and Peter, and Phoebe served the church in Cenchrea (Rom. 16:1). Some deacons would by temperament be best suited to continue in this role, but many, having learned all they could from an apostle, prophet, or administrator, would move on to greater responsibility. This was often the case in the Middle Ages when a bishop had an archdeacon as his assistant. The archdeacons so often succeeded their "master" that it was considered more suitable for them to be ordained priests and counted above the level of the parish clergy. Anglicans continued the same system, and left the rank of "unarch" deacon as a mere stepping stone to the priesthood. It is time that confused tradition gave place to a true understanding of the function of deacon, which would involve a recovery of the apprenticeship system as the essential part of ministerial training and

---

[2] Gibbs and Morton, *God's Frozen People*, p. 162.

the seminary as an option for those who could benefit from academic studies.

As with the other gifts of the Spirit, there is a wide range of "deacon" or service functions in the body of Christ (Rom. 12:7; I Cor. 12:28). We saw that the gift of teaching might be at the Sunday School level, or as a full-time congregational "rabbi," in conventional Bible ministry, seminary instruction, or even as an international figure known to the masses through books, radio, and television. There will be an equally wide range of personal assistants, deacons, secretaries, and helpers of various kinds in the Christian church.

We should begin with the servants needed in a local congregation. Until a Christian finds himself developing a particular gift, he can in any case start by helping wherever help is needed. We are not speaking of social service in the community, which we looked at in Chapter IX. Here service is assisting in one of the functions of the church, making possible or at least easier the work of preaching, administration, works of mercy, or finance. Nor do the gifts of deacon and helper have anything to do with attending committees. The current fashion is to assume that no one will do anything useful unless he is set to sit and plan. All this does is to exhaust the available membership and thoroughly frustrate those who know that God has called them to work, as opposed to discussing the work. Service is helping a gifted person to exercise his or her gift in the church. It is doing, not discussing.

The real servant begins by asking the questions, "What is God doing in this congregation? Who is being used of God to do it? How can I help the persons God is using?" This means that the gift of helpers must not be made into an office, or special title; least of all can it be a place that needs to be filled every year by voting. A church may need full-time or part-time secretaries, janitors, bookkeepers, librarians, mailing-list clerks, men's and women's group conveners, and the like; but the gift of helpers is not to be confined to a tidy name. It is an active giving of oneself to be of assistance to the work of God. If the duties are hard or routine, unnoticed by the public eye, lacking in glamor or financial remuneration, it is still a gift of the Spirit, precious in God's sight and held in regard by the one who knows how to judge rightly. In God's sight there are no inferiors and superiors, and reward does not depend on the acclaim of men. God does expect us to perform our function in the right place and at the right time, and one of these functions is service, which is no different in quality from any other gift, though it does differ in kind.

Our next chapter discusses the bloodstream, the mission of the church. Here also we need our personal assistants and helps. If God is evidently using Paul, John Wesley, William Carey, or Billy Graham, the first priority is to insure that they are given all the help that they can use. If the modern church should find a prophet capable of communicating to the masses, it is a great honor to serve him as personal assistant or secretary. In many overseas missionary situations there are men of God who have mastered the language, gained the confidence of the people, and are in great demand as teachers for a growing national church. Unfortunately as new missionaries arrive, the experienced missionary is expected to reduce his work to serve the newcomers. This may be an evidence of great grace on his part, but one can imagine what kind of success an army would have if the brilliant general would give himself to solving the little problems of his junior officers rather than having their help to press on to victory.

Thirteen

Body and Bloodstream

We come at last to mission, the lifeblood of the body of Christ. Mission is our major concern, but the preliminaries had to be discussed, since all mission is the product of local churches. If sending congregations are deficient in spiritual gifts, missions also will be anemic; and where missions fail to function, the churches in turn will suffer. Moses already knew what modern medicine is rediscovering — that "the life of the flesh is in the blood," "the life of every creature is the blood of it" (Lev. 17:11, 14). In Chapter VI we used Paul's analogy of the variety of cells in the human body to illustrate the variety of functions in the church. These functions are what make up our local congregations, the relatively fixed bones and muscles and tissues of the body. The bloodstream is distinct, although it is related to the local church at every point. Its distinction is that it moves to give life to the whole.

The purpose of blood is to bring oxygen, vitamins, food energy, repair materials, hormones, and much else to provide what is needed for health. In the Christian church this corresponds partly to what has been called mission, though the term mission has been too restricted. "Missions" are often assumed to be overseas, exotic, patronizing, and colonial, with an emphasis on savage tribes, the underprivileged, and certain back-door concerns such as slums, alcoholics, addicts, Eskimos, and Indians on the reservation.

In this chapter and the next we shall look at the bloodstream functions illustrated in the New Testament. At the outset it should be clear that this is no distinction between home and foreign, privileged and underprivileged. The bloodstream goes wherever the body is. Mission is what moves to give life to the church everywhere. In modern-day situations it includes Billy Graham and the traveling evangelists and teachers, student movements like Inter-Varsity, S.C.M., and Campus Crusade for Christ, Sunday School organizations, conference and retreat centers, which though fixed obviously minister to the whole body. To these we must also add the seminaries and Bible colleges, Christian writers and radio programs, the Bible societies and translators, as well as most of what is usually called missions. All these can be distinguished clearly from local congregations, which have their own responsibility and are in fact the front line of the church. The laymen of these congregations are touching the world at every point. They are the infantry in close contact, and they occupy the ground that is captured. The bloodstream brings them the ammunition and supplies, the materials needed to repair the breaches, and the trained specialists to assist them in their task.

The neglect of the bloodstream has been the major cause of flabbiness and weakness among Protestants. It has been the strength of the Roman Catholic Church. On the one hand there are the parish congregations linked together through priests, bishops, and archbishops in every country. They are fixed and occupy the ground. Quite distinct is the Roman bloodstream that is rich with Jesuits, Dominicans, Franciscans, Marians, Knights of Columbus, and a host of other orders. These may have special emphases and they may concentrate more particularly in certain areas, but they are essentially worldwide in outlook. They are not confined to foreign countries, as most Protestant missions have been, but they keep watch on the whole body, giving specialists and other assistance wherever there is an opportunity of growth, or the need of repair, or evidence of sickness in the Roman Church.

By its very nature the bloodstream cannot be controlled; least of all can it be confined in the local parish structures. The Roman orders at home and Protestant missions overseas have learned that it is not their business to interfere in local church administration. If converts are won they must be left to organize themselves in local churches that are independent of mission control. Any ministry within local churches must be by invitation, and should not continue too long. On the other hand the orders long ago discovered what Protestant missions are now learning painfully, that missions cannot be placed under the permanent control of local congregations or even synods. Parishes are meant to be parochial in outlook, and missions are meant to look to the interests of the whole body; neither can control the other.

The failure to understand this basic theological distinction between denominational structures and missions is the root of the present confusion in the ecumenical movement. Beginning with the assumption that denominations should be united, or at least in a state of oneness so that dialogue can take place, the movement foolishly concluded that separate missions did not fit. The logical outcome was the dissolution of the International Missionary Council and its incorporation in the hierarchical structure. The theory was that there would be no more missionaries, but instead fraternal workers would go from one group of churches to work under another group. This serious mistake in strategy has only recently been discovered. If the unity of the body of Christ is to be promoted, it must be tackled in two distinct ways. First, the aim should be to attain intercommunion, free transfer of membership, and free transfer of ministers at the local level. The other need is to encourage inter-mission cooperation in the bloodstream by such things as the use of a common Bible, mutual recognition and cooperation among seminaries, and the sharing of literature, know-how and experience. Within the bloodstream there will inevitably be hundreds of mission agencies and orders, and ways must be found for local congregations to know what these have to offer and take what they need from each.

To arrive at this concept of the body of Christ some drastic changes are needed in our theology of the church. By its very nature the bloodstream is interdenominational since it ministers to the whole body. As we saw, the evangelist will be frustrated if he is forced to make Anglicans or Baptists out of his hearers.

The Bible teacher cannot say, "I will only teach those of my own denomination." He has to teach wherever men need to be taught and are willing to listen, whether he is invited to a Pentecostal church or to the Vatican. To some extent the best radio preachers and theological and devotional writers already have an audience right across the spectrum of denominational groupings. To extend this approach would require churches to release their best men into the bloodstream to feed, strengthen, heal, and repair the body of Christ regardless of denominational or even geographical boundaries. Ordinary church members are already very free privately to read the books and hear the preachers of other denominations. Local churches will need to learn how vital it is for them to draw what they need for their life from the missions in the bloodstream.

This will have financial implications, as we shall see in Chapter XVI. At present most Protestant, Roman Catholic, and Greek Orthodox hierarchies will only allow parish contributions to their own denominational agencies. Some denominations are so narrow that they will only recognize their own little missionary society, as if that were the only richness in the bloodstream of the body of Christ. In this respect the Anglicans of England are by far the most worthy of praise. There is no official Anglican missionary society, and every parish church is free to give to any of the twenty or more Anglican societies as well as to an unlimited choice of interdenominational groupings. This freedom has enriched the parishes greatly, and it has made possible the retention within the Church of England of a range of theological and ecclesiastical opinions unequaled in any other church. In other countries the Anglican churches have pathetically tried to insist on the channeling of all missionary giving through their one national Anglican missionary society, except that in Australia two Anglican societies, one high and one low, are given official recognition. Roman Catholic parishes have a wide choice of Roman orders to support, but the day might come when some interdenominational groupings will also be allowed. Similarly there is tight missionary control through Presbyterian general assemblies. One overseas and one home mission are usually specified, and it is the assembly that passes every detail of the budget.

This raises the question of control, which has been a constant bone of contention between the bishops and the orders of the Roman Church. As we have seen, a simple answer is to say that, though the bloodstream is entirely the product of local churches, it can never be controlled by them, nor does it control the churches that it establishes. We can see this clearly in Paul's churches. It would have been fatal for Paul's movements to have been directed by Antioch or by the churches he founded in Galatia. On the other hand the churches that Paul founded could, if they desired, refuse his ministry and transfer their allegiance to other teachers. There was a mutual independence and mutual interdependence, as in the human body, between the bloodstream and the organs and tissues. We shall look at this in more detail in the next chapter, where we deal with the function of apostles as leaders of mission teams.

Before concluding this chapter we should include within the bloodstream the various institutions that the church's life keeps on creating. In many parts of the world the first hospitals, colleges, schools, and other social service organizations were initiated by Christians. As these were organized, the question of control had to be decided. Sometimes they were put under a local church or diocese or denomination, but more often they were established under independent boards or societies. Several centuries of experience have proved that church control has grave disadvantages, since both the controlling church and the controlled institution are likely to suffer. Every extra administrative headache makes concentration on the real work of the church more difficult. Agendas become so burdened with buildings, budget, and salary-scale problems that spiritual vision for the evangelistic and pastoral task is dimmed. High-pressure administrative experts are required, while ambitious men must seek office in the church structure if they are to control the institutions. Institutions also suffer because the otherwise excellent parish pastors and presidents of ladies' organizations that parishes like to elect, know little about the administration of specialized institutions.

The other alternative is to set up a self-perpetuating board. In Britain this system was adopted for the colleges in Oxford and Cambridge, the great hospitals in London, the best known boarding schools, and most of the theological colleges. A similar impressive list could be prepared for the United States, including most of the Ivy League universities and the leading institutions of most cities. The advantage of this system is that it allows freedom to develop new institutions as they are needed, and freedom from a heavy load of administration, so that the church can concentrate on evangelism, pastoral shepherding, and spiritual needs. In our analogy the institutions of the church come under the bloodstream rather than under the denominational organizations. They are admittedly fixed in location, but a typical church-founded college touches so many parishes that it can in no sense be called local. There is of course the objection that the self-perpetuating board may eventually fall into wrong hands, but this is the fate of all human organizations, including churches. The acceptance of this principle would have saved many headaches in overseas missionary situations, where small struggling churches were saddled by well-meaning missionary societies with vast colleges and hospitals. If missions in the bloodstream wish to establish good works in any place, they themselves should run them, or, better, put them under self-governing boards that do not burden the shepherds and sheep of the nearest congregations.

We hear much of the sin of a divided church, but I wonder how the Lord, the head of the body, views the problem. He is in touch with every true Christian in every congregation of every denomination, so that there is in any case one body. For all these he has one bloodstream, and individual Christians take more from that one bloodstream than most of us realize. Jesus Christ's problem is freedom rather than unity. Local cells need to be freed to cooperate with the next cells. Congregations should feel free to take from the bloodstream regardless of denominational labels. Movement from local churches into bloodstream ministry could be freed from unnecessary administrative and financial controls. If all Christians were free to be themselves, the one body would be healthier. Denominations might continue as a good way of grouping Christians, and a rich number of orders and missions will be required for the bloodstream. Outsiders will be impressed by the abundant vitality of the body, rather than the tidy mergers of its denominations. Since life is what we need, we could go back to Moses to learn that "the life of the flesh is in the blood," which is why I believe in missions.

Fourteen

Apostles and Teams

The apostolic function is the most neglected and yet most necessary gift for the worldwide church. The higher churches maintain that apostles were replaced by diocesan bishops in the apostolic succession. Evangelical Protestants say that apostles died out with the New Testament era. Most Christians learn about the twelve apostles' in Sunday School, but have never heard of apostles today.

We can begin by listing certain agreed propositions. Obviously the function of the twelve disciples of Jesus, often called the twelve apostles, can never be repeated. They were chosen to be for three years eyewitnesses of everything that the Messiah did until his death and resurrection. Eleven of these men continued to be available for several years after so that anyone might question them concerning the facts. For this purpose a twelfth apostle was chosen to replace Judas. These twelve men could give eyewitness evidence concerning the real humanity and sinlessness, the real crucifixion, and the visible resurrection of the Messiah so that these facts could not be controverted by any amount of cross-examination in any court of law. I suspect that the number of honest doubters who went and did this questioning for themselves was considerable. It was, after all, the Romans who gave us the principles of eyewitness evidence, and even before Romulus and Remus Moses had taught the Jews the modern principles of legal proof.

The second agreed proposition is that Paul was an apostle, but in no sense could he qualify as one of the original twelve eyewitnesses. When the dispirited disciples wanted to choose a successor for Judas the choice had to be "one of the men who have accompanied us during all the time that the Lord Jesus went in and out among us, beginning from the baptism of John until the day when he was taken up from us" (Acts 1:21f.). It is true that Paul saw the Lord on the Damascus road, but this evidence was irrelevant compared with the basic historical facts that the twelve eyewitnesses could give about Jesus' life and death and resurrection. What happened to Paul on the Damascus road has happened to many converted persecutors of the church; and it still happens, because Jesus Christ is alive and knowable face to face today.

Our third proposition is that the Greek word *apostolos* originally meant a naval expedition; later it referred to the commander of a naval force; and by New Testament times it could be used for any responsible person sent to do a particular task for the sender. Every day hundreds of apostles traveled across the Greek and Roman world. Ambassadors went to establish an outpost at a foreign court, businessmen were sent to open new branches, and Christian apostles fanned out to win and organize churches for their Lord. The word apostle was therefore not confined to the twelve, who were in a special sense the eyewitness apostles, but was applied also to men like Paul, Barnabas, Andronicus, and Junias, and even to false apostles who tried to perform the same function.[1]

The fourth proposition is that Paul twice lists apostles among the other gifts of the Spirit, and both times places this at the top of the list. "And his gifts were that some should be apostles, some prophets, some evangelists, some pastors and teachers" (Eph. 4:11f.). "God has appointed in the church, first apostles, second prophets, third teachers" (I Cor. 12:28).

Finally we have the fact that Paul's function, quite apart from the question of his office, was to be the leader of a team

---

[1] See Acts 14:14; Rom. 16:7; II Cor. 11:5, 13.

(commander of an expedition, in the classical Greek sense) responsible for planting churches and discipling them for Jesus Christ. This function of planting and discipling churches is the function that is deficient and desperately needed in our twentieth century.

Now if these propositions are generally agreed upon, why is there such divergent teaching on the apostolic function among our theologians? One reason was the emergence of the big city bishops in the second and third centuries, as we saw in Chapters II and III. To maintain control over the ordinations in their area it was easy to suggest that bishops were successors to the twelve apostles, so that no man could become a priest without a valid ordination by a bishop in the true apostolic line. If, however, we adopt the distinction between local churches and the bloodstream, the connecting of apostles with a continuing line of bishops is not necessary. The essence of the catholic tradition can be maintained by recognizing apostles with their mission teams or orders in the bloodstream, and at the same time having the local parish churches organized under bishops. This in fact is what does happen in the Roman Catholic Church in many areas, though the apostolic nature of the orders is not recognized.[2] As Roland Allen saw clearly in China, the Anglican system must be adapted to permit the ordination of elders in newly founded churches without a long theological training. What he did not stress was that the church-planting missionary should be an apostle who hands over these new churches to the church organization in the area, and then moves on to plant other churches without retaining responsibility for or authority over them. It would be a major theological breakthrough for our theology of church and mission to allow for apostles and mission teams on the one hand, and local churches organized under bishops, presbyteries, conferences, or something similar on the other hand.

We now come to the problem from the Protestant or Evan-

---

[2] See for example the otherwise first-class treatments by the Maryknoll Fathers, *The Modern Mission Apostolate,* ed. William J. Richardson; and Joseph A. Grassi, *A World To Win: The Missionary Methods of Paul the Apostle.* Both these books use the word apostolate, but never define the apostle's function in relation to diocesan bishops.

gelical side. Here the issue is the canon of the New Testament. Whereas the "Catholics" continue the function of apostles wrongly, the great Reformation theologians ended it with the New Testament. They held that the church is apostolic in the sense that it is ruled by the New Testament writings. If apostles are continued beyond the apostolic era, then how can we close the canon? Will not modern apostles begin to add new parts of Scripture in the twentieth century? By this reasoning it is taken as axiomatic that apostles and prophets died out by the end of the first century, and that their Word of God is the New Testament, to which nothing can be added. The result is that Protestant churches have been very seriously impoverished, except on the mission field overseas, by the lack of apostolic bloodstream ministry.

The question of the New Testament canon needs a separate treatment, but it seems quite unnecessary to terminate the necessary function of apostles in order to establish it. In any case the apostolic nature of Paul's epistles, of the epistle to the Hebrews, of James, of Jude, or even of the Gospel of Mark, is impossible to prove if we have to connect these writings with the original twelve apostles. It is far simpler to agree that the New Testament canon was planned and terminated in the same way as the Old Testament canon by the predestination of God. It is a miracle of history that all Jews and all Christians agree about all the books of the Hebrew Old Testament.[3] Similarly it is an even greater sign of the hand of God that all Christians, whether Roman, Greek Orthodox, Syriac, or Protestant, agree about the New Testament canon. It is this unanimity that is conclusive, not the supposed evidence that our New Testament books were written by the twelve apostles or under apostolic authority.

Once the problem of the canon can be removed from the discussion of apostles, it might be possible to recover a real

---

[3] The Roman Catholic Apocrypha was never in Hebrew, never quoted in the New Testament, and never adopted as canonical by the Jewish Council of Jamnia which settled the Old Testament canon for ever. The addition of the Apocrypha from the Alexandrian Septuagint Greek version is an accident of history, but it does not affect the absolute agreement concerning all the books of the Hebrew Old Testament.

apostolate in twentieth-century Protestant churches. First, the existing denominational missionary societies need to be freed from hierarchical control for a more mobile bloodstream ministry both at home and abroad. Then it is necessary to search for men with apostolic church-planting gifts, and make it possible for them to exercise this ministry. As men begin to move in this way, interdenominational and inter-mission teams will probably form, and local churches will learn to take from them what they need. When these teams begin to plant new churches, the existing denominational groupings will need to learn how to recognize their elders and ministers, and link the churches in fellowship with others. If we remember that apostles and bloodstream teams have no ecclesiastical authority once self-governing churches are established, it seems unnecessary for local denominational groupings to be jealous of the labors of apostolic teams.

Evidently the problem is not to invent new ways to make the church relevant to the twentieth century, but to recapture the vibrant life and mobility of the early Christians. How, for example, do we produce a Paul? Let us assume that our theology of the church has progressed to the point where we do not have to expel a John Wesley from our church because his apostolic gift has no place in our tradition. Let us also assume that our understanding of the apostolate is so enlightened that we can now accept a new congregation, or ministry from an apostle of another denomination and still remain ourselves. Then how do we recognize the apostolic gift? Our textbook is already written. God has carefully set the pattern in the New Testament.

At his conversion on the Damascus road, Paul immediately received his inward call to the apostolate. "I have appeared to you for this purpose, to appoint you to serve and bear witness to the things in which you have seen me and to those in which I will appear to you, delivering you from the people and from the Gentiles — to whom I send you to open their eyes, that they may turn from darkness to light and from the power of Satan to God, that they may receive forgiveness of sins and a place among those who are sanctified by faith in me" (Acts 26:16-18). The inward call was not recognized outwardly for at least fourteen years until Paul went out on his first missionary journey. He began by acting as an evangelist wherever he had an opportunity to preach. Then he spent many years in Tarsus and the surrounding province of Cilicia. When the church in Antioch began to grow at a rapid rate, Barnabas went to Tarsus to call Paul to help in teaching the converts. The future apostle was sent to Jerusalem on a famine-relief mission, and he presumably heard of the work of other apostles and gained a wider picture of God's plan for the worldwide church.

These fourteen years of preparation gave Paul his theological training and practical experience in the exercise of various spiritual gifts. We must recognize that, whereas most of us are one-talent men, there are others in the church with two or more spiritual gifts. Usually to qualify as an apostolic leader of a mission team, a man will need to have developed evangelistic, teaching, and administrative gifts. Paul obviously had these, and he also spoke in tongues and had a gift of healing. He was at least a five-talent man. Inevitably as he began moving in the Mediterranean world his gifts and leadership were recognized, younger men joined him, churches backed them, and the team enriched the Christian bloodstream in the Roman world.

Paul's labors are singled out in the book of Acts and in the epistles, but other apostles led other teams, and their combined efforts exploded a vast Christian population east as well as west of Jerusalem in the first three centuries. If the true church of Jesus Christ is to grow faster than the twentieth-century population explosion, which I assume to be God's intention, we will need to produce, recognize, and use Pauline apostles. If theology or ecclesiology makes that impossible in our little circle, God will still work, but not through our cancerous stupidity. *I will build my church, and the gates of hell shall not prevail.* Those hellish gates are built by tradition as well as worldly wickedness.

Fifteen

Clergy and Laity

The picture we have drawn of the early church includes local churches with an abundance of spiritual gifts and apostolic teams moving in the bloodstream. We have wondered how it would do as a blueprint for today. What then shall we say of the ordained ministry? If all Christians are to exercise a gift, should all be ordained ministers, as among the Jehovah's Witnesses? It was well said about the early Society of Friends that the idea was not to have no ministers, but to have no laymen. Should we stop ordaining? Or should we ordain everybody?

From another angle we must ask which members of the body of Christ should be paid, or be in so-called full-time ministry. If some should be paid, how much and by whom? An American humorist once defined a minister as "a good man hired by the wicked to prove to them by his constant example that righteousness does not pay." Who should hire or fire ministers, for what purpose, and on what basis? Evidently the questions are thorny: one chapter will answer little and satisfy less. Anglicans and Roman Catholics, Brethren and Friends, and all in between, will be hurt unanimously.

Ordination generally takes place by the laying on of hands. Roman Catholics require a bishop in the apostolic succession; Anglicans claim the same succession but include the hands of other priests with the bishop. Presbyterians ordain by ministers without a bishop. Baptists use deacons, who are really elders, for the same function. In some denominations there are representatives from other churches at the ordination, and it has even been insisted that every member of the local congregation participate in it. In any case the person being ordained is recognized, indicated, and given new authority by the laying on of hands. The higher Anglicans, Roman Catholics, and Greek Orthodox add that something priestly is also imparted by the proper hands in the proper ceremony.

Like most Christian activities, the roots of ordination lie firmly in the Old Testament. The Jews used the laying on of hands to designate or indicate a person or animal for a particular function. If a man brought a sin offering he laid his hands on the head of the lamb. What was meant by this was: "This is my lamb. I deserve the penalty, but this innocent victim takes my place: Lord, have mercy on me a sinner" (Lev. 4:24, 29; 16:21; Num. 12:8). The patriarchs laid hands on their children to indicate the blessing that was destined for them (Gen. 48:14-20). Moses laid hands on Joshua to appoint him as successor (Num. 27:18-20). David Daube gives evidence that rabbis used to lay hands on their disciples to ordain them for the same work, and that this practice was continued in the early church, so that it became accepted that a bishop could ordain his successor.[1] That the laying on of hands was not confined to ordination for church offices is clear from the fact that Jesus laid his hands on children and on the sick, as did the apostles. It was also used in connection with prayer for the receiving of the Holy Spirit. Evidently the laying on of hands was not restricted to the ordination of ministers or elders for a local congregation, since it is evident that Barnabas and Saul were appointed for missionary service, and Timothy was ordained for a function in the mission team by this ancient sign.[2]

It is therefore obvious that the laying on of hands was used

---

[1] David Daube, *The New Testament and Rabbinic Judaism,* pp. 207-208.

[2] See Acts 9:17; 28:8; 8:15-17; 19:6; 13:3; I Timothy 4:14; II Timothy 1:6.

for a wide variety of functions in both the Old and New Testaments. We saw in Chapter II that local churches like the synagogues that preceded them were free to make their own rules according to the degree of organization that they had attained. In the worldwide church today we must also allow each church or grouping of churches to use the laying on of hands for as many functions as they find appropriate. Whether they decide to "ordain" full-time teachers only, or all teachers, including Sunday School teachers, or the men who are authorized to administer the bread and wine, or only one man per congregation who is to be "The Minister," or go the whole way and ordain all who hold any office in the church — these things must be decided by whatever wisdom the church can muster. Whatever we do, let there be some logic that can be explained to the ordinary man. I would also plead for a sensible understanding of the practice of ordination or the lack of ordination in other groups and a respect for equivalent functions. For example, if one denomination lays hands on theologically trained itinerant Bible teachers, and another does not, can we not agree to recognize the species rather than question the validity of the rite of recognition?

I would ideally like to see two kinds of laying on of hands. At the local church level the laying on of hands by representatives of the congregation could be used to designate all elders, deacons and deaconesses, and also to commend missionaries leaving the congregation to go into the "bloodstream" ministry of the church universal (see Chapter XIII).

There would also be a denominational laying on of hands where a trained and approved teacher, evangelist, prophet, pastoral counselor, or administrator is designated for a wider ministry, whether at the local church level or in the "bloodstream." After ordination in this way he would still have to be accepted either by a local congregation or by an order or mission team to work with them. Just as a local church or mission team has to maintain a list of its own workers, so each denomination would maintain a list of its approved "ordained men" for a wider ministry. I hope that the practice of extending denominational approval to those ordained by other groupings will also become more common.

In this way churches could be encouraged to recognize the gifts of the Spirit among their members, and also the gifted men available in neighboring churches and in the various "bloodstream" teams. The safeguard is that any local church is responsible for testing and if necessary refusing the ministry of any teacher, evangelist, prophet, or pastor, whether or not he is on the "ordained list" of a denomination, if he does not have the marks of a man of God. This principle of testing by the local church is clearly taught in the New Testament.[3] It is not sufficient that a preacher should have had a good training or be on the denominational roll, since it is clear that many of the New Testament false teachers began in good standing in the church. If every local church felt responsible to test those who came to preach and refused to hear again those who brought heresy or a wrong spirit, it would be comparatively easy to maintain the doctrine of the church.

We have not yet discussed the question of whether ministers should be paid or unpaid, full-time or part-time. If ordination is to be used by a local church to commission the gifted persons who serve it, and if it is also used at the denominational level to recognize various approved workers, then obviously the question of whether or not a man is paid to do these jobs is irrelevant. As in the early church, there will be an army of gifted persons exercising their functions as teachers, pastors, evangelists, elders, deacons, and in other good works; and most of these will be earning their own living. Their profession is the wave-length by which they are known in society, but their gift is the medium through which they communicate Jesus Christ to the community.

For the first three centuries of church history the vast majority of elder-bishops seem to have had their own means of livelihood. But the church will always need a number of men and women, both at the local level and in the bloodstream, who will give themselves to exercising their spiritual gifts on a full-time and therefore salaried basis. In some cases these may move in and out of so-called full-time service. On Paul's first missionary

---

[3] See Gal. 1:7-9; II Cor. 11:13-15; II Pet. 2:1-3; 3:17; I John 2:18-23; 4:1-3; II John 7-11.

journey, and on his second journey up to the time of his arrival in Corinth, he never stopped to earn his own living. Most likely he used funds provided by his friends in Antioch. Paul tells his churches that they should provide finance for their teachers (Gal. 6:6; I Tim. 5:17; I Cor. 9:8-12). Even Jesus accepted financial support from his followers (Luke 8:3). How many persons should be supported partly or in full by local churches will vary according to circumstances. It is in any case a matter of economics rather than theology.

Let us imagine a church growing from the very first converts in a new area. Whether this is in Africa or Britain, in a primitive tribe or in Chicago, among middle-class suburbanites or industrial workers, it makes little basic difference. When ten or twelve families have begun to meet they can be constituted as a congregation. Among these the leaders will become obvious, and as soon as possible elders should be designated. As Roland Allen pointed out from his experience in China there is no need for these men to be sent away for elaborate theological training. Any mature Christian man who is respected in the community should be able to conduct a simple communion service or share what he has learned from personal Bible study. Paul ordained elders very soon after the first churches were founded in Galatia, and we do a disservice to church growth by following any other method.[4]

As the church grows and the elders consider its spiritual needs, it may become obvious that one of their number could do much more if he were freed from having to earn his own living. He might, for example, concentrate on pastoral visitation or devote a few months to putting up a church building. Later as the giving of the members increased, it might be possible to have a full-time deaconess to work among the women and children and for the service of the community. The next step could be a missionary project to send a Timothy, a Mark, or a Silas to join a mission team. If the church grew to the point where it could take on a theologically trained "rabbi" to teach its members and help teach other struggling churches in the

---

[4] Acts 14:23; see Roland Allen, *Missionary Methods: St. Paul's or Ours?*

area, there would then be the equivalent of our twentieth-century seminary-trained minister, the difference being that he is not *the* vicar, *the* parish priest, or *the* pastor. Nor would he necessarily have to give himself to sitting on committees, running the administration, or even be chairman of the session. This could be done by others gifted in these directions, and his task would be to devote himself to the study of the Word of God, teaching in the congregation, communicating with intellectuals, refuting error, and perhaps pursuing a writing and radio ministry. Instead of bypassing the parish ministry in large numbers, the best theologians and teachers might be challenged and recaptured for the work they are trained to do.

Such an approach to part-time and full-time ministry could deliver us from the ridiculous idea that a church must hire a man who has all the gifts, and that his success is measured by how many "laymen" can be persuaded to attend his activities. The idea of the one-man ministry became entrenched in the Middle Ages, when the lord of the manor hired a priest to care for the religion of his subjects. The one-man ministry was further strengthened, instead of being reformed, at the Reformation, and it has only been seriously questioned by such groups as the Anabaptists, the Quakers, the Plymouth Brethren, and in our own day by the Pentecostal assemblies. The sixteenth century rediscovered Paul's doctrines concerning faith, and today many Roman Catholic theologians agree that Luther also was a true doctor of the church. It might be even more significant for the growth of the body of Christ in an exploding world population if the twentieth century rediscovered Paul's view of the gifts of the Spirit to provide the ministry required for true congregational life.

Before closing this brief discussion of the ordained ministry, we should note in passing its relationship to the celibacy of the clergy. That Paul expected most local church elders to be married is obvious (I Tim. 3:2; Titus 1:6). It is generally agreed that many presbyters and city bishops of the first three centuries were family men. The movement towards celibacy began with the asceticism of St. Antony (*ca.* 251-356) and the early Egyptian monks. That monks should be celibate was laid down by Buddha and also by Mahavir, founder of the

Indian Jains, in the sixth century B.C. The practice was adopted by the Essenes and in the famous Qumran monastery in the two centuries before Christ. If strong-minded monks and gentle nuns are to live in ascetic communities, they have to be celibate. How then did a necessity for monks become a rule for all the ordained clergy? The article "Celibacy of the Clergy" in the *Oxford Dictionary of the Christian Church* provides a short answer. At the Council of Nicea (325) a proposal by the Egyptian monks that all clergy should be compelled to give up living with their wives was decisively rejected. At the Council of Trullo (692) the eastern branches of Christendom decided that priests and deacons could marry before ordination, but not after; and only unmarried priests were allowed to be made bishops. In the west a decretal of Pope Siricius (386) ordered celibacy for "priests and Levites." On ordination the practice throughout the Middle Ages was for a married man to send his wife to a nunnery. In 1917 the Roman Catholic Church finally forbade the ordination of a married man by *Codex Iuris Canonici,* but the present revolt indicates that the question is by no means settled.

For Protestants the question has been carelessly settled by implying that all men should be married, that celibacy is unfortunate, that bachelors are suspect and spinsters to be pitied. Jesus Christ clearly indicated that for the sake of the kingdom of heaven some disciples will renounce marriage voluntarily; and Paul said that in unsettled situations to be single is an advantage (Matt. 19:10-12; I Cor. 7:25f.). The celibate Roman Catholic orders and not a few outstanding individual Protestants have demonstrated that for some tasks unmarried men and women have tremendous advantages. There are also innumerable cases where the cause of Jesus Christ would have been helped if young men had delayed the responsibilities of sex relationships until basic studies were behind them and they were settled into their life work. As it is, the average North American Protestant male is emotionally and sexually involved with girls from his early teens; he is married when he should be sharpening his mind with other men in university; and he is immobile with children when he could be out staking the claims of the church in unfamiliar ground. That celibacy is required as a qualification for the service of Jesus Christ is monstrous. That so few adopt celibacy, at least for a period, as a means to an end is tragic.

As we have noted before, both in the Bible and in the church, the truth often lies at once in the two extremes. Celibacy is good and marriage is good, and both have their right places. Christians called to a settled work in a local situation will usually be more effective if married. This includes most men in the so-called ordained or parish ministry. Many of those called into the bloodstream of the body of Christ would profit from voluntary celibacy, at least for a time. For some tasks unmarried men and women are needed, but, as Paul warned, "each has his gift from God" and it is certainly "better to marry than to be aflame with passion" (I Cor. 7:7-9). For special tasks there should be orders like the Jesuits and Dominicans that require celibacy for their members, but if any of these marry later there is no reason why they should be disqualified from being licensed to a parish ministry. A similar system already works effectively in some of the Anglican orders where marriage may terminate membership in the order, but does not exclude from continued usefulness in a parish situation.

Celibacy was an interesting tangent from our subject in this chapter. If churches consist of gifted persons performing a variety of functions in a local situation, and the bloodstream consists of apostolic teams moving to nourish, stimulate, and repair the body, then what is the meaning of clergy and laity? The honest answer is that they have no meaning. This does not, however, mean that ordination is meaningless. Every church and denomination must use the outward sign of recognition, the laying on of hands, to express what they intend to indicate. Men and women can be ordained by the laying on of hands for various functions, but that does not elevate them from laity to clergy. Ordinations may be more frequent, clergy could be dispensed with; all Christians can be invited to work but none will be laymen. How each denomination can rediscover the New Testament is difficult to visualize. To expect uniformity of practice is foolish. To understand the practice of others is wise. To use all the gifts given by Christ to build his church is in any case imperative.

Sixteen

Tithing and Giving

One of the disasters of the Middle Ages was the rigidity introduced by the land tithe. In Britain by A.D. 900 one-tenth of the produce of most of the agricultural land was exacted by the church. Giving to God had become a tax rather than a willing expression of loyalty. Worse than this was the fact that the lord of each manor could appoint a rector, who received the tithe of the parish as his salary. If part was appropriated for other uses, the parson was called a vicar; but in any case on appointment he obtained "a living," or the right to his share of the tithe as long as he performed his ecclesiastical duties in that parish. This was called the parson's freehold. For rigidity, spiritual obtuseness, and moral injustice, it is hard to think of a system further removed from the genius of Christianity.

There is nothing wrong with tithing as a way of providing the salaries of Christian workers. God enjoined one-tenth as the basic principle of giving in the days of Moses, though it was already established in practice in the days of Abraham and probably long before (Gen. 14:17-20; Lev. 27:30-32; Num. 18:21-24). Jesus Christ rebuked the hypocritical church leaders of his day for tithing the little shoots of mint and dill and cummin in their gardens, but then neglecting "the weightier matters of the law, justice, mercy and faith." Obviously tithing is no substitute for righteousness, nor does it enable us to earn our own merit before God. It does provide a most simple and effective way of paying the salaries of religious workers without the tedious folly of entertaining and cajoling the faithful in the hope that they will be persuaded to meet the budget. In rebuking the failure to concentrate on the major items of righteousness, Jesus indicated that he expected the tithing in any case to continue. "These you ought to have done, without neglecting the others" (Matt. 23:23f.).

Books on stewardship and tithing are available, so it is not necessary to press the argument that Christians ought to tithe, or at least give a regular proportion of their income. It might be helpful to consider how this could be administered in a modern situation. In the United States and Canada the governments consider it reasonable for a man to give a portion of his income to charities. For example, the U.S. allows a man to reduce his gross income up to twenty percent for gifts to charities and an additional ten percent for gifts to churches. In Canada a similar system prevails. The taxpayer must be able to produce proper receipts for such deductions. In Britain the system is much more cumbersome, through deeds of covenant, which commit the giver to giving to a particular charity for seven years. Unless an individual is paying tax at the full rate the business of making the covenant hardly seems worth the bother. A good case might be made for arguing that if charitable organizations in Britain grouped together to persuade the government to change the income tax laws to the North American system, both the number of givers to charity and the total given would multiply enormously.

Now let us assume that the serious giver has decided how much he is going to give to charities per month or per year. Some sects and churches expect him to give virtually everything through the church budget, while at the other extreme there are givers who so distrust their church administration that they give a minimum in the offering and dispose of the rest themselves. On the average a reasonable sum might be half one's tithe through one's local church, and the remainder for other charities. This would mean that twenty to twenty-five families in a congregation could support a full-time family man at their average salary, and fifty families could pay a minister and build a simple church. This still leaves the other half of the tithe for investing in other good works and the worldwide "bloodstream" of the church.

Before turning to the how of investing we should note that Paul also speaks of the "gift" of giving. *He who contributes, in liberality* (Rom. 12:8). This is not the ordinary giving according to one's income, or the tithe that we have discussed, but an additional gift of giving. This is the man who is no preacher, but earning more than he needs; he lives simply and gives himself to investing heavily in the work of God. Writing about the richer members of the community, Paul says to Timothy, "They are to do good, to be rich in good deeds, liberal and generous." One part of this gift of giving is the willingness to live simply as one's income increases. The other part is to invest in the growth of the body of Christ as wisely as one would invest in secular enterprises. It requires discerning what God is doing in the world, understanding how Christian work is done and then encouraging what is worthwhile. Obviously the work of Jesus Christ can never make much impact in our exploding populations without very heavy investment of this kind. Just as in the human body some cells have the task of channeling energy wherever it is most needed, so the Holy Spirit apportions the gift of giving for this purpose in the body of Christ.

It now becomes evident that control in the church lies with those who give. At the local level congregations can form and grow where there are families who give for the operational needs of their church. If the church ceases to perform its function or diverges into error, the ordinary member need not be helpless, since it is his giving that ultimately makes the work possible. Similarly it is his decision to invest or not to give the other half of his tithe that governs what is done by the Christian church in the community and throughout the world. It was the lack of individual responsibility that made the compulsory tithing system of the Middle Ages so iniquitous. Similarly today the "laymen" of the church should never permit the organization men of the denominational hierarchies to build up large investment endowments, since these have the same effect as a compulsory tithe in taking control away from the individual Christian and vesting it in the organization. The church should live on its income, and the income comes from the members who believe in it.

On the wider scale of the outreach of the church among the nations it is the heavy givers, those with the gift of giving, who will exert most control. To understand the most pressing opportunities for church growth, and act decisively in a highly mobile situation, is probably beyond the capacity of the average church member. This is where the wise businessman, who is also filled with the wisdom that comes from God, can and should have a decisive influence. To attain this quality of giving on a world scale will require a ruthless ignoring of the tear-jerking appeals, the pathetic pictures of need, and the immature heroism that has marked so much of our missionary effort. If investment in an industrial enterprise merits careful study, a summing up of the markets, an estimate of the capability of the directors, and a scrutiny of the accounts, how much more the work of God?

One objection to this type of control through the freewill giving of every Christian family is that the pressure of money may cause a minister to lose his prophetic voice. If his living depends on satisfying the people, will he not be tempted to compromise his message? If a missionary society grows or contracts according to the whim of those who give to it, will it not be forced to concentrate more on public relations than on preaching the gospel? One answer to this is to make sure that every minister or missionary is able to earn his own living by having his own profession. When tempted to compromise he can remind himself that he is not ultimately dependent on those who pay him. Jesus Christ accepted financial support so he could preach, but everyone knew he could also earn his living as a carpenter. When insufficient income came from his churches, Paul did not need to give his time to public relations. He knew how to support himself, and his whole missionary team if necessary (Acts 20:34), by his ability in the tent-making business.

The corollary of the need for every Christian worker to have his own profession is that the existing system of requiring many years of specialist theological training is unreasonable. If theologians are required, they can equally well be trained as philosophy professors, historians, or classical linguists; and a short additional reading course in theology, church history, or New Testament Greek should be sufficient. Some of the best theologians have in any case been competent in the secular university disciplines. If professional pastors are to be trained, there is no reason why they should not qualify themselves as psychiatrists, or sociologists, or educational counselors. Most denominational organizations would profit by recruiting their administrators from the ranks of business executives who are also dedicated Christians. Missionary societies would do well to take journalists, salesmen, publishers, teachers, philosophers, linguists, doctors, agriculturalists, anthropologists, and advertising men, who had proved themselves as Christians in the secular world. After a short course in the message that needs to be communicated, followed by intensive study of the language and culture in the country where they are to work, such men should be able to communicate Christian truth and establish outposts for Jesus Christ as well as, if not better than, most of our existing missionaries. If the church wishes to be secular to communicate to a secular world, is not the first requirement to train its workers in secular professions? If the objection is that such men might fall into theological error through lack of years of theological studies, the answer is that they can hardly fall further than our present crop of theologians.

A more serious objection is that if the church's most dedicated men and women are going to train in the secular world, will there not be an acute shortage of so-called full-time Christian workers? For a time there might be fewer in terms of numbers, but the influence of these dedicated persons both during and after such secular training might not necessarily be less. At present the main challenge for Christian service is to the young, whereas a challenge to the experienced might be even more productive. The most telling argument is that if Jesus Christ trained as a secular carpenter and Paul as a tentmaker, and none of the early Christian missionaries had long years of theological training, and yet they did so much, might not a similar experiment at least be worth trying?

So far we have spoken of control through finance, and

financial independence through professional training. There is, however, another truth, an opposite truth, that also needs to be kept in focus. More things are wrought by prayer than this world dreams of. Ultimate control, or rather the power of creative initiative in the Christian church, comes through prayer. In the human body the organism can only grow and the muscles act if sufficient energy is provided. The opposite truth is that no creative activity is possible without decisive will power. Energy alone is ineffective, and there can also be a will to act without the calories to make it possible. Of the two, will is by far the more important, since will can often find the calories, and where there's a will there is usually a way. So in the church. There are those with a gift of giving who provide the proteins and calories without which the body of Christ would be im- mobile. There are also those who pray; often they are the more penniless members of our congregations. The men and women who know how to discover the mind of Christ and then pray accordingly, they are the ones who move mountains, open closed doors, shut the mouths of lions, and bring captivity captive among the nations. For some marvelous reason the creator has chosen to let things be done when insignificant men and women pray. This is why it is also true that a missionary society that has praying supporters is more rich than one that depends on wealth alone.

Einstein taught us that energy can be changed into matter, and matter redissolved into energy. We are beginning to learn the power of will over matter, and it may be that ultimate energy is in fact only will in space-time form. The church certainly needs financial giving for a greatly increased ener- gizing of the body of Christ in the world. We are his hands, his feet, his mouth, his heart, his eyes; and apart from us he chose to be silent and unseen. But more than anything we need nervous energy, creativity, decisive willing according to his will, and that is the gift of prayer. Paul calls it *dunameis,* the moun- tain-moving gift. Like all the gifts, every Christian experiences it to some extent on some occasions, but blessed are those who kneel to will according to the will of God.

Seventeen

Present and Future

"Then tell us what to do. Where do we go from here? I am more confused than when you began. Why not leave us alone? At least our pews are comfortable, though the world may be lost." And the clergy join the chorus. "We are tired of diagnosis and blueprints and quacks. We may be paid too little, but at least it comes every month, and we have a roof over our heads. Laymen are difficult enough as they are, without having them trying to run everything and then leaving us to pick up the pieces. We would love to see the vitality of the New Testament, but meanwhile we have to cope with what there is. We would do things differently if we were starting again, but better the organization we now have than the chaos you are creating. It is all very well for you to write from your study, but come and show me what you would do here."

Why not begin with facts, or rather the fact of God, the living God, the God of Abraham, Moses, David, Peter, Paul, and John. He is wise and his plan is perfect. We can also take his church as a fact. His Son is building more gloriously than Solomon, and there are a surprising number of new living stones for the new temple being assembled throughout the world. The gates of hell may threaten, but they are less likely to prevail than nineteen centuries ago. At its best the church has been magnificent. The blood of the martyrs, the women facing the beasts of the arena, the Roman senator and his slave sharing the bread and the wine, the taming of the savage tribes of Europe and the equally savage tribes of today, the Pilgrim Fathers, the schools, the universities and hospitals where men were free to think and to love, Wilberforce and Shaftesbury, the Salvation Army, St. Francis and Pope John, some faithful pastors among the hypocrites, occasionally an intensity of love and fellowship, and most of all the first evidence that the poor and dull and insignificant are important as people. When these things were seen ordinary men suspected that perhaps God was there after all.

With the obvious facts we also need the theological facts. God is not in a hurry as we are. The most Christian of men are very imperfect this side of heaven. There are many tares among the best of wheat. The growth of life both in nature and by the spirit is imperceptible, and what is to be is never seen. The end product is the City of God. Its design is perfect. It only awaits the people who are still being fashioned in this space-time world.

Having accepted the facts of a God who works and the imperfection of the men that he uses, we can begin with the congregations that we have. The Christian radical does not root up everything. Rather he goes to the root of the matter to discern what can become a flower. He is a conservative in the sense of retaining everything that is good. He removes the obvious weeds, and knows that a garden is not grown in a day. The Christian radical is also a teacher. Rather than criticize, he has great faith in steady instruction. At least all Christians should know that the gifts of the Spirit are various, and God is pleased with variety. We may disagree on the meaning of some of the gifts, but we could start by encouraging those whose meaning is obvious. Sunday School and Bible class teachers can be recognized and encouraged to give themselves to excellence in teaching the Bible. We already have elders, parish council members, or boards; and these persons could be helped to see that the gift of spiritual administration can be more than church politics. We must pray that God will give us all the gifts that we need, and then be grateful when they appear.

To clarify the practice of ordination will take a long time. There is obviously much of value in every denomination that needs to be conserved. As radicals we can, however, begin asking what exactly we mean by the laying on of hands, and which functions should be designated in this way. The best changes are made in line with precedent and by small, almost imperceptible steps. If we know what we are trying to achieve, it is surprising how much can be changed before the radical nature of a transformation is noticed.

Re-creating the anemic bloodstream of the church is an immediate priority. Missions and orders are already in existence. They need to be recognized as the very life of the body, the source of all that God provides to give energy, repair damage, fight disease, and initiate growth throughout the world. Local churches and the denominations in which they are grouped must be helped to take of the richness that the bloodstream has to offer, and in turn be willing to give the Timothys and Pauls and Lukes and Johns that the blood requires.

Most of all we need a vision of the church as the body of Christ, its growth throughout the world, and the tremendous purposes that Christ as its head has in mind. This is a vision that can excite men to live dangerously, and suffer and die to make the vision visible on earth as a prelude to its perfection in the City of God.

What of the future? Marshall McLuhan's great theme is that since the Gutenberg printing press man has learned to extend himself mechanically. His hands extended into tools, production lines, and giant earth-moving equipment. His feet extended their pace with automobiles, rockets, and jets. Now in the twentieth century man is extending himself electronically. Fifty years ago virtually all of man's mental operations were carried on inside his brain. Now large numbers of men have extended their brains electronically into computers. Man's nervous system has already been tremendously extended by telegraph, telephone, radio and television. Now the link-up between computers all over the world, and the rapidly multiplying instant connections from brain to brain, seem likely to create a kind of global consciousness. Whether or not McLuhan is right in prophesying that this is going to take us back to tribal man is questionable. For the Christian, McLuhan's ideas may suggest a further stage of development in the church as the body of Christ.

So far the church has taken root in many countries and in widely different cultures. Until recently these national and tribal churches were isolated. Their only connection was through missionary members of the bloodstream who began to move more rapidly to distant parts in the eighteenth century. Even in one country parish churches were parochial. Now the electronic link-up noticed by McLuhan is inevitably going to bring Christian congregations throughout the world into close contact. It is as if the body of Christ is now developing a unified nervous system. Already Billy Graham in London has been shared simultaneously by hundreds of churches through closed-circuit television channeled via the telephone system. In North America he is seen and heard by millions of viewers on coast-to-coast television systems. We should expect the church to produce other worldwide figures with other prophetic, evangelistic, and teaching gifts.

As global instant communications develop we can already see Christians of all denominations beginning to think and feel as one. This unity will not be a linear organizational[1] unity, such as took place in the bureaucracies that united the British Empire. Rather it will be an instant electronic or nervous unity such as exists in the human body. Christians do not feel one by connecting up through denominational hierarchies that are then united administratively. They could conceivably be one by seeing each other on television, hearing the same preachers, responding the same way, praying together, giving for the same causes, and sensing the common enemy. Such opportunities for unity will be vastly increased by Telstar television, supersonic jets, and communications satellites round the world that may soon make telephone conversations the same price regardless of distance.

Beyond the electronic future for the church, there is the ultimate future when space-time will have been left behind and we shall know as we are known. Meanwhile God has graciously

---

[1] Again using one of McLuhan's categories. See *Understanding Media*.

given us death, the death of every parent and lover and child, and our own death in particular, as a means for us to see our existential decision. In any case there is no meaning in this world as it is. Either I must say that there is no meaning and there never can be, which is nihilism, or I can say that there is no meaning but I will have faith in myself as the only giver of meaning, or I may say there is no meaning now, but that I believe in a superman or a superstate that will one day give this world a meaning. Or I can be a Christian and say, "I believe in Jesus Christ, the only giver of meaning, God-man, who chose to give me meaning out of my meaninglessness. He is the head of the body, the church, in which I have a function until my task is done." Death then loses its sting, life has its joyous excitement, and other men and women become people rather than things, subjects instead of objects, fellow citizens of the city that has foundations, whose builder and maker is God.

Bibliography

The following books are listed for further study. The titles marked with an asterisk most influenced my thinking. For the rest, together with large numbers of periodical articles, conference talks, and discussions with friends, I can only say that I am indebted to many more than I can remember.

*Allen, Roland. *Missionary Methods: St. Paul's or Ours?* Grand Rapids: Eerdmans, 1962 (first publ. 1912).

*————. *The Spontaneous Expansion of the Church and the Causes Which Hinder It.* Grand Rapids: Eerdmans, 1962.

*————. *The Ministry of the Spirit: Selected Writings of Roland Allen* (ed. David M. Paton). Grand Rapids: Eerdmans, 1962.

Andersen, Wilhelm. *Towards a Theology of Mission.* London: SCM, 1955.

Anderson, G. H. (ed.). *The Theology of Christian Mission.* New York: McGraw-Hill, 1961.

Berton, Pierre. *The Comfortable Pew.* Toronto: McClelland and Stewart, 1963; Philadelphia: J. B. Lippincott, 1965.

Blauw, J. *The Missionary Nature of the Church: A Survey of the Biblical Theology of Mission.* London: Lutterworth, 1962.

Boer, Harry R. *Pentecost and Mission.* 2nd ed. Grand Rapids: Eerdmans, 1961.

Bromiley, Geoffrey. *The Christian Ministry.* Grand Rapids: Eerdmans, 1959.

Brown, J. A. C. *Techniques of Persuasion.* London: Penguin-Pelican, 1963.

*Bruce, F. F. *The Spreading Flame.* Grand Rapids: Eerdmans, 1953.

*Calvin, John. *Institutes of the Christian Religion.* 2 vols., tr. Ford Lewis Battles; ed. John T. McNeill. Philadelphia: Westminster, 1960.

Catherwood, H. F. R. *The Christian in Industrial Society.* London: Tyndale Press, 1966; Chicago: Inter-Varsity, 1966.

Congar, Yves. *Lay People in the Church.* Rev. ed. Westminster, Md.: Newman, 1965.

*Cox, Harvey. *The Secular City: Secularization and Urbanization in Theological Perspective.* New York: Macmillan, 1965.

*Cross, F. L. (ed.). *The Oxford Dictionary of the Christian Church.* London: Oxford, 1958.

118

Bibliography

*Daube, David. *The New Testament and Rabbinic Judaism.* London: Athlone, 1956.

*Davis, Merle J. *New Buildings on Old Foundations.* New York: International Missionary Council, 1947.

*Dix, Gregory. *The Shape of the Liturgy.* Naperville, Ill.: Allenson, 1964.

The Documents of Vatican II (ed. W. M. Abbott). New York: Association, 1966.

*Dodd, C. H. *The Apostolic Preaching and Its Development.* New York: Harper, 1936.

*Eusebius. *Ecclesiastical History.*

Foster, J. *Beginning From Jerusalem.* London: World Christian Books, 1956.

*Gibbs, Mark and Ralph Morton. *God's Frozen People.* London: Collins-Fontana, 1964; Philadelphia: Westminster, 1965.

Glover, R. H. and J. H. Kane. *The Progress of World-wide Missions.* Rev. ed. New York: Harper, 1960.

Grassi, Joseph A. *A World to Win: The Missionary Methods of Paul the Apostle.* Maryknoll, N. Y.: Maryknoll Publications, 1965.

*Gwatkin, H. M. *Early Church History to A.D. 313.* London: Macmillan, 1909.

Hanson, Anthony T. *The Pioneer Ministry: The Relation of Church and Ministry.* London: SCM, 1961; Philadelphia: Westminster, 1961.

Harris, Paul T. (ed.). *Brief to the Bishops: Canadian Catholic Laymen Speak Their Minds.* Toronto: Longmans Canada, 1965.

*Hastings, James (ed.). *Dictionary of the Apostolic Church.* 2 vols. New York: Scribner, 1916-1918.

————. *Encyclopaedia of Religion and Ethics.* 13 vols. New York: Scribner, 1951.

Hatch, E. *The Growth of Church Institutions.* London: Hodder & Stoughton, 1881.

*Hay, A. R. *New Testament Order for Church and Missionary.* Audubon, N. J.: New Testament Missionary Union, 1947.

Henderson, Ian. *Power Without Glory: A Study in Ecumenical Politics.* London: Hutchinson, 1967.

Hogg, W. R. *Ecumenical Foundations: A History of the International Missionary Council.* New York: Harper, 1952.

*Hooker, R. *Treatise on the Laws of Ecclesiastical Polity.* 2 vols. New York: Dutton (Everyman's Library 201, 202).

*Hort, F. J. A. *The Christian Ecclesia.* London: Macmillan, 1900.

Hudson, Winthrop S. *Religion in America.* New York: Scribner, 1965.

James, Walter. *The Christian in Politics.* London: Oxford, 1962.

Jenkins, C. and K. D. Mackenzie (eds.). *Episcopacy, Ancient and Modern.* London: S.P.C.K., 1930.

The Church: An Organic Picture of Its Life

*Judge, E. A. *The Social Pattern of Christian Groups in the First Century*. London: Tyndale, 1960.

Kilbourn, William (ed.). *The Restless Church: A Response to The Comfortable Pew*. Toronto: McClelland and Stewart, 1966; Philadelphia: Lippincott, 1966.

*Kirk, K. E. (ed.). *The Apostolic Ministry*. New York: Morehouse, 1946.

Kraemer, Hendrik. *A Theology of the Laity*. London: Lutterworth, 1958; Philadelphia: Westminster, 1959.

*Kung, Hans (tr. Cecily Hastings). *The Council, Reform and Reunion*. New York: Sheed and Ward, 1961.

————. *Structures of the Church*. New York: Nelson, 1963.

Lacey, T. A. *The One Body and the One Spirit*. London: J. Clarke, 1925.

Latourette, K. S. *A History of the Expansion of Christianity*. New York: Harper, 1937-1945.

Levy, Isaac. *The Synagogue: Its History and Function*. London: Vallentine-Mitchell, 1963.

Lietzmann, Hans. *The Beginnings of the Christian Church*. London: Lutterworth, 1955.

*Lightfoot, J. B. *The Apostolic Fathers*. Grand Rapids: Baker, n.d.

*————. *Dissertations on the Apostolic Age*. London: Macmillan, 1892.

*————. Dissertation on "The Christian Ministry," in *St. Paul's Epistle to the Philippians*, pp. 181-269. Grand Rapids: Zondervan, 1957 (first publ. London: Macmillan, 1900).

*Lindsay, Thomas M. *The Church and the Ministry in the Early Centuries*. London: Hodder & Stoughton, 1902.

*McGavran, Donald A. *The Bridges of God: A Study in the Strategy of Missions*. New York: Friendship, 1955.

*————. *How Churches Grow: The New Frontiers of Mission*. New York: Friendship, 1959.

*———— (ed.). *Church Growth and Christian Mission*. New York: Harper, 1965.

McLuhan, Marshall. *The Gutenberg Galaxy*. Toronto: University of Toronto, 1962.

*————. *Understanding Media*. New York: McGraw-Hill, 1964.

*Marcel, Pierre. *The Biblical Doctrine of Infant Baptism*. Naperville, Ill.: Allenson, 1953.

Marty, Martin. *Church Unity and Church Mission*. Grand Rapids: Eerdmans, 1964.

*Nee, Watchman. *Concerning Our Missions*. Grand Rapids: Zondervan, 1939.

*Neill, Stephen. *A History of Christian Missions*. London: Penguin, 1964; Grand Rapids: Eerdmans, 1965.

Bibliography

———— and Hans-Ruedi Weber (eds.). *The Layman in Christian History.* Philadelphia: Westminster, 1963.

*Nevius, John L. *The Planting and Development of Missionary Churches.* Philadelphia: Presbyterian and Reformed, 1958 (first publ. 1885).

Nichol, John Thomas. *Pentecostalism: A History of a Religious Movement.* New York: Harper, 1966.

Niebuhr, H. Richard. *The Social Sources of Denominationalism.* New York: Meridian, 1957 (first publ. 1929).

Oesterley, W. O. E. *The Jewish Background of the Christian Liturgy.* Repr. Magnolia, Mass.: Peter Smith (first publ. 1925).

*Paton, David M. *New Forms of Ministry.* London: Edinburgh House, 1965; New York: Friendship, 1965.

Philips, G. *The Role of the Laity in the Church.* Notre Dame, Ind.: Fides, 1955.

*Phillips, J. B. *Letters to Young Churches.* New York: Macmillan, 1947.

*Pickett, J. W. *Christian Mass Movements in India.* Nashville: Abingdon, 1953.

*————. *Christ's Way to India's Heart.* Narberth, Pa.: Livingston, 1938.

Pittenger, W. N. *His Body the Church.* New York: Morehouse-Gorham, 1945.

————. *The Church, the Ministry and Reunion.* Greenwich, Ct.: Seabury, 1957.

Ranson, C. W. (ed.). *Renewal and Advance: Christian Witness in a Revolutionary World.* London: Edinburgh House, 1948.

*Renwick, A. M. *The Story of the Church.* London: Inter-Varsity, 1958; Grand Rapids: Eerdmans, 1959.

Richardson, William J. (ed.). *The Modern Mission Apostolate: A Symposium.* Maryknoll, N. Y.: Maryknoll Publications, 1965.

————. *Revolution in Missionary Thinking.* Maryknoll, N. Y.: Maryknoll Publications, 1966.

Robinson, J. A. T. (ed.). *Layman's Church.* Naperville, Ill.: Allenson, 1963.

Robinson, William. *The Biblical Doctrine of the Church.* St. Louis: Bethany, 1948, repr. 1963.

Ryrie, C. C. *The Place of Women in the Church.* New York: Macmillan, 1958.

Sanford, Agnes. *The Healing Gifts of the Spirit.* Philadelphia: Lippincott, 1966.

————. *The Healing Light.* St. Paul, Minn.: Macalester Park, 1957.

Shearer, Roy E. *Wildfire: Church Growth in Korea.* Grand Rapids: Eerdmans, 1966.

Shedd, Russell P. *Man in Community: A Study of St. Paul's Application of the Old Testament and Early Jewish Conceptions of Human Solidarity.* Grand Rapids: Eerdmans, 1964.

*Soltau, T. Stanley. *Missions at the Crossroads.* Grand Rapids: Baker, 1955.

*Stewart, John. *Nestorian Missionary Enterprise: The Story of a Church on Fire.* Edinburgh: T. & T. Clark, 1928.

*Stibbs, A. M. *God's Church: A Study of the Biblical Doctrine of the People of God.* London: Inter-Varsity, 1959.

Streeter, Burnet H. *The Primitive Church.* London: Macmillan, 1929.

*Swete, H. B. (ed.). *Essays on the Early History of the Church and Ministry.* London: Macmillan, 1918.

Tawney, R. H. *Religion and the Rise of Capitalism.* London: Penguin-Pelican, 1938 (first publ. 1926).

Telfer, William. *The Office of a Bishop.* London: Darton, Longman and Todd, 1962.

Thornton, L. S. *The Common Life in the Body of Christ.* 4th ed. Naperville, Ill.: Allenson, 1963.

Troeltsch, Ernst. *The Social Teaching of the Christian Churches* (tr. Olive Wyon). 2 vols. New York: Macmillan, 1956.

Vidler, Alec R. *The Church in an Age of Revolution.* Grand Rapids: Eerdmans, 1964.

Visser 't Hooft, W. A. (ed.). *The New Delhi Report: The Third Assembly of the World Council of Churches.* New York: Association, 1962.

*Warren, M. A. C. *The Christian Imperative.* London: SCM, 1955.

Webster, D. *Patterns of Part-Time Ministry in Some Churches in South America.* London: World Dominion, 1964.

Why the Sea Is Boiling Hot: A Symposium on the Church and the World. Toronto: United Church of Canada, 1965.

World Christian Handbook. New York: Friendship, 1962.

39-200